UNSHAKABLE
DESTINY

UNSHAKABLE DESTINY

FROM TRAGEDY TO TRIUMPH

WILL BOGGS

XULON PRESS ELITE

Xulon Press
2301 Lucien Way #415
Maitland, FL 32751
407.339.4217
www.xulonpress.com

Living Waters Ministry
4803 Old Vashti Road
Hiddenite NC 28636
828-632-3906

Printed in the United States of America.

ISBN-13: 978-1-54566-813-9

Acknowledgements

I would like to thank my mom and dad Lee and Denise Boggs for all their contributions to my life, ministry, and book. Without there love and support and the platform of Living Waters Retreat Ministry has provided I would not have been able to write a book or be at the place I am at in my life and ministry today.

Thank you so much to my wife Mariah Boggs. Without your unconditional love, support, and encouragement, I would not have been able to complete this book or be the father and husband I am today. I love you so much and am so blessed to have the most precious jewel as yourself to be my wife and the mother to Elizabeth and our future children.

I am grateful to Jason Borneman for helping me with getting all my pictures and promotional videos for the book and also for helping with some editing for it and promoting it.

Thank you Dr. Pete for your support of
my family, ministry, and your forward.
I'm so honored to be your friend and
to have you forward my book.

Thank you Dory Abbott, Dee Worley,
Nelson and Karina Delanuez
for your contribution to the editing of my book.

Thank you so much to everyone who
endorsed my book including Alex Kendrick,
Darius Daniels, Bishop Michael Badger,
Pastor Stephen Ward, Dr. Reginald McDaniel,
Dr. Dean Simpson, and Pastor Chris Meade.

CONTENTS

FOREWORD

They said, "He's Dead! It's impossible. He will Never..."

I can understand, life has a way of doing that to all of us!! Even the most well intentioned professionals and the kindest and most well meaning friends and family, can get caught up in the reality of this world that bombards our senses and our lives each and everyday. This is never more apparent then in the throws of real tragedy & insurmountable odds.

It is why, my great friend Will's story is so inspiring. His story is a story of FAITH. A mother's faith, a father's faith - a community that came together and determined NOT to lose perspective NO MATTER WHAT!!!

The privilege of our new lives in Christ is to walk by FAITH - a DIVINE impartation & realization of the reality of Heaven in our lives. It is the understanding that we are heirs (citizens) of God, representations of Jesus Christ on the earth. We are in the world, but not of this world. This natural world is no longer our reality - HEAVEN IS!!!

We win life's battles... By standing on TRUTH & walking by FAITH

I love what the Apostle Paul articulates to the Believers at Corinth, "For though we walk in the flesh, we do not war according to the flesh. For the weapons of our warfare are not carnal but mighty in God for pulling down strongholds, casting down arguments and every high thing that exalts itself against the knowledge of God, bringing every thought into captivity to the obedience of Christ," II Corinthians 10:3-5 NKJV

Paul gives us the example of how to live this life when he chose to know nothing but Jesus Christ and Him crucified.

"For while I was with you I was determined to be consumed with one topic — Jesus, the crucified Messiah." 1 Corinthians 2:2 TPT

Why? Jesus is the reality of our NEW life as children of God.

"We look away from the natural realm and we fasten our gaze onto Jesus who birthed faith within us and who leads us forward into faith's perfection..." Hebrews 12:2 TPT

Jesus is our perspective & the filter by which we live out our lives!

The GOSPEL consumes us & defends us in every situation.

"Unshakeable Destiny" is the GOSPEL lived out through Will's incredible story...

Bless you!
Dr. Pete Sulack
StressRX.com

"I've met Will Boggs and have seen his incredible witness with my own eyes. This story will not only strengthen your faith, but remind you that our God is able to do far more than we could ever think or imagine. This book is stunning!"

-Alex Kendrick
Writer/ Filmmaker

It has been said that it's not what happens to us that defines us but rather our interpretation of those events and whether that interpretation is empowering or disempowering. In this amazing work, Will Boggs walks you through his personal journey and offers awesome insight into how God helped him discover his purpose in the midst of pain. This work is a powerful picture of possibilities if we are willing to embrace the truth that God really does work all things together for our good and his glory.

-Dr. Darius Daniels
Change Church, Ewing, NJ

Having the privilege to meet Will and his beautiful family, his story is our modern day Lazarus. Will's story will bring you to tears as well as laughter it will cause your faith to soar to new levels it will confirm what the bible has told us "all things work together for our good". This book is a must read!

-Bishop Michael Badger
Bethesda World Harvest International Church,
Buffalo, NY

Embedded in my memory forever, is the day a young teenager stood, apologizing for having notes to guide him in sharing his story, told how in a terrible car-truck wreck, he was pronounced dead on the highway, shocked into a heartbeat by an emergency helicopter crew, existed in coma for weeks and the physicians finally wanted to turn off all life support and let him go. Nurtured by the faith in God of his parents and simple gifts placed in the special glyconutrients present in plants by God, he like another centuries ago, rose from his death bed to live a life serving others. My decades of research on the power of more comprehensive nutrition has never been more richly rewarded, the purpose of my life fulfilled, than in the celebration of the restored life of Will Boggs.

-H. Reg McDaniel, M.D.

I have been deeply impacted by Will's journey of faith and his miraculous testimony of being raised from death to life. His life and story will encourage you to believe God in a deeper way and embrace a lifestyle of miracles. I pray you will be immensely blessed by this book just as I have been tremendously blessed by Will's life.

-Stephen Ward
Pastor of The Living Room Movement

What would you change in your life if you could go from "Life – to – death – to – life" again? Will Boggs has lived this experience and through the mercies of Jesus Christ gives testimony of His Grace. I recommend Will's book to you. It will encourage the discouraged and challenge the contented. Read it and be blessed!

-Dr. H. Dean Simpson
Director: Helping Hands Ministries,
Statesville, N.C.

"Will Boggs is an outstanding young man who is allowing God to do amazing things through him. He has an incredible story of tragedy, trials, and triumph! He is a captivating speaker who uses an abundance of scripture to reveal God's tremendous work and healing in his life. I am excited about this book and the countless lives that will be encouraged by it."

-Pastor Chris Meade
Crosspoint Church, Taylorsville, NC

INTRODUCTION

After a horrific car accident involving an eighteen-wheeler, I plunged head first into a forty-day coma. All reports declared I would not make it through the first night. As you read my amazing story, you will see how my tragedy turned into triumph. You will see how God works all things together for our good, transforming our lives in the midst of the most tragic situations.

My name is William Boggs IV. You can call me Will. After a tragic car accident, the God of Miracles brought me back to life. During the coma, the resurrection life of Jesus surged through my body. God sent His Word and healed me as my family declared the Word of God in faith over my broken, paralyzed body for forty days. I am convinced that God brought me back with powerful keys that will unlock anyone who finds themselves in a hopeless situation. I was reported as a fatality after our car was hit by an eighteen-wheeler. I was airlifted to a trauma center, and for the next forty days, my life was hanging by a thread. Machines kept my body organs functioning. As I lay in a comatose, lifeless state, my spirit was more alive than ever. On the outside, I appeared lifeless, but on the inside, I was alive and screaming out to my family for help. Had I been locked up in a hospital room? Was I being held as a hostage somewhere?

No, I was locked up inside my body. The impact of 250,000 pounds of pressure was too much for my body to withstand, so it shut down into a coma. Even though I was in a coma, I was very much aware of what was going on. What I discovered during those forty days was a powerful revelation that will unlock anyone who feels shut down due to tragedy or a traumatic event.

During the next forty days, my family prayed and read the Word of God over me twenty-four/seven. When the Word is declared by faith, the power of God is released. God's will for my life was written in His Word, and my body responded according to my unique design.

Although I was in a coma, I could still hear and feel the impact of God's Word as it was being declared. As the Word surged through my soul and saturated my spirit, healing took place in my body. It was like when the dry bones that responded and came together when Ezekiel prophesied to them in Ezekiel 37. Our body, soul, and spirit were created to respond to the Word of its Creator.

The Bible talks about how being absent from the body is to be present with the Lord. I guess you could say God spoke to me during this time and encouraged me through different circumstances, as I came out of the coma. On one such instance, He gave me a glimpse of my future. This glimpse gave me the faith, hope, and strength to keep fighting and persevering each day. Even when I came out of the coma and was paralyzed and strapped to a wheelchair, I held on to the hope that I would walk again.

The whole process of being trapped in my broken, paralyzed body during the coma made me feel like I was trapped in a cocoon. The Greek word for "transform" from Romans 12:2 and 2 Corinthians 3:18 is *metamorphoo,* which has the same meaning as metamorphosis. As I was crying out to God to be released, God was transforming me, preparing me to fly to higher heights than ever before. God is the God of miracles, and as you read this book and pray through each prayer, you too will be taken to a higher level of faith to be able to hope for the impossible things in your life to be possible.

Day after day, talking with God is how I got to know Him as my Father, as my Healer, and as the only One who could reveal the purpose for why He created me. He revealed to me that for anyone to fulfill their destiny, their spirit has to be fully awakened. The same God that brought me back to life and infused me with purpose can bring you back to life from whatever tragedy you have gone through.

I pray your spirit will be awakened to embrace God's purpose for your life as you read my story, *Unshakable Destiny*.

Will

Chapter 1

SPRING BREAK BROKEN

The journey to find my purpose began as a fifteen-year-old teenager on spring break.

During this time as a freshman, I became greatly concerned about the direction of my life and wondered what my purpose was. The morning of March 25, 2005, I began reading the *Purpose Driven Life* by Rick Warren. I was certain this book would answer my questions. Little did I know that finding purpose is a journey—a marathon, not a sprint. I thought that I could make the journey of finding purpose on my spring break vacation. But after placing a bookmark at the end of the second chapter, I would not pick the book up again for several years. It's not that I was no longer interested in the book and what it said about finding purpose, but at that instant, my life would come to a screeching halt.

Within seconds after I closed the book, a semi-truck traveling at sixty-five miles per hour crashed into our family SUV and t-boned us as we crossed a four-lane highway. The last thing I can remember before it happened was asking my mom if I could just read the book straight through over my week-long spring break vacation, rather than reading it for the suggested forty days.

I don't recall every detail that happened that day, but my mom got out of our SUV to buy some strawberries, then got back in the car to continue our drive to visit my grandparents in Cape Coral, Florida. It was a rainy, cloudy, and dark evening, so visibility was poor. My sister, an eighteen year old, was driving. As she was attempting to pull out of the fruit stand, a parked semi-truck was blocking her view. The driver of that parked truck waved his hand to motion that the way was clear. That was the hand motion that changed our lives forever.

My mom saw the motion and said, "Wait, you can't see!" But with the second signal from the man, my sister trusted the truck driver and pulled out. Our SUV was hit by another oncoming semi-truck. We were t-boned right behind where I was sitting, on the side of the gas tank.

The semi was traveling at the full speed of sixty-five miles per hour, knocking our car across the road into the median. The crash was so loud that the fruit stand owner heard it and ran toward our vehicle. He was the first to arrive at the accident scene. He shouted to his wife, "Call 911!" When the man got a closer look, he yelled, "I don't think the boy in the backseat is alive." He was horrified at the sight of blood pouring out of my nose, mouth, ears, and even out of my eyes!

The paramedics had just finished a call close by, so they arrived in just two minutes. As they approached the scene of the accident, they didn't expect to see anyone alive. Accidents involving semi-trucks on this highway were common and usually involved fatalities. The paramedics worked quickly, with the knowledge that the gas tank could explode at any moment. They found my mom unconscious in the front passenger seat. My sister was conscious and bloody with glass embedded in her face and her lips lacerated, but when they tried to pry her out, she screamed, "No! No! Help my brother! He's not breathing!" The paramedics had to pry me out of the SUV. They laid me out on the side of the road. They couldn't find any vitals, but because my teeth were clenched, they couldn't use the respirator. One of the paramedics quickly did an emergency tracheotomy to get some air into my lungs. The ambulances, police cars, and other emergency response vehicles arrived at the scene soon after. As soon as the helicopter arrived, the paramedics put me in, and the helicopter lifted off for the nearest hospital in Gainesville, Florida.

I mentioned before that the weather wasn't good, and visibility was awful. As the helicopter headed toward Gainesville Hospital, a massive, black storm cloud formed in front of them. Later they told my parents it was like a massive brick wall that they couldn't penetrate. They were forced to turn the chopper around and fly in the opposite direction towards SHANDS Trauma Center in Jacksonville, Florida.

I now know that the massive storm cloud they faced was put there by God to keep them from going to the wrong hospital. Gainesville Hospital was not equipped to treat a brain injury as severe as mine. At the time, SHANDS Trauma Center was the only hospital in the southeastern part of the US with the medical equipment required for the procedure I needed. I had to have a hole drilled into my skull and a bolt inserted to drain fluid off my brain. Had I gone to Gainesville Hospital, they would not have had the equipment to drain the fluid off. However, the helicopter pilot had to make this decision quickly in the air without informing my parents. My mom and sister were taken by ambulance to Gainesville Hospital.

My mom had regained consciousness in the ambulance. As she awoke, she knew what had happened, and she was beside herself searching for me. My sister was in the ambulance with her, but I was not. The paramedics told her we would all be reunited at Gainesville Hospital. No one knew the helicopter had been rerouted.

Once my mom and sister arrived at Gainesville Hospital, my mom immediately asked to see me, but no one at the hospital recognized my name or knew what she was talking about.

Gainesville Hospital frantically called neighboring hospitals, but there was no sign of William Boggs. They called SHANDS Trauma Center in Jacksonville, but again, my name was not registered there.

My mom was in a panic — where was I; what had happened to me? She didn't know if I was alive or dead. It was soon discovered that I was at SHANDS Trauma Center. When the chopper left the scene of the accident, they did not get my name; they had me listed as "John Doe."

After a lot of back and forth, SHANDS Trauma Center reported they had admitted a fifteen-year-old "John Doe." My mom had to describe me to them to confirm that "John Doe" was in fact her son. They informed her that I was in critical condition, on life support, and that she had to come as soon as possible because they couldn't perform the procedure to drain the fluid that was crushing my brain without her physically identifying me.

The hospital quickly arranged for a taxi to carry my mom to SHANDS Trauma Center in Jacksonville. The drive from Gainesville to Jacksonville was two hours, and every second counted. It was ten o'clock at night, and my mom had to ride with a complete stranger for the two-hour drive. She had a fractured sternum, no cell phone battery, and no way of contacting my dad, while overcome with anxiety about two of her children. She had to leave my sister, who was being taken to surgery, to be with her other child in worse conditions. She tells the story that the moment she got into the taxi, she said, "I don't know if you believe in God, but I do and I'm crying out for Him to save my son." The taxi driver turned around and said, "Yes Ma'am, that's why I am here!"

My mom arrived in Jacksonville and confirmed she was the mother of "John Doe." They now had the go-ahead needed to drill the hole in my skull and insert the bolt to drain the fluid off my brain. By this time, my head was swollen to twice its size from all the blood and fluid accumulated around my brain.

There is no record of how long my mom sat in the dark waiting room waiting to hear the outcome of the procedure. As she waited and cried out to God, a hospital chaplain came in to be with her. The chaplain's support in prayer was undoubtedly needed as my mom faced the next blow. The surgeon came in and said, "Mrs. Boggs, I have some bad news. Your son arrived here in a level-three coma. He's got immense swelling on his brain. Even if we get the fluid off of his brain, the more critical problem is that from all indications, his brain appears to have been severed from the brainstem." He went on to say, "The body cannot sustain the impact of 250,000 pounds of pressure and survive."

He then made a motion with both hands, showing how my brain had separated from the stem. At that report, the chaplain could not stand it another moment; she stood up, pointed her finger upward, and said, "*But my God is a very present help in time of trouble, and He is here!*"

Without another word, the surgeon walked away. Remember, when the Word of God is spoken in faith, powerful things can happen. When my mom heard the encouraging scripture from the chaplain, she was greatly encouraged. She felt invigorated with a new hope that God had not abandoned her son.

When the procedure was completed, I was taken to a hospital room. Hours had passed with my mom having no word from my dad, but as my mom and the chaplain were walking to my room, she saw my dad coming down the hall. They were reunited at my door, even though they had not talked since early that morning when we left for the trip to Florida.

When my dad heard my mom's voicemail, he jumped on a plane as fast as he could. With that information, he traced our steps from the fruit stand, made multiple calls, and flew to Jacksonville without ever talking to her.

They walked into my room, hand-in-hand, as they faced the most shocking sight of their life. My head was so swollen that I was unrecognizable, with eighteen tubes running into my ears, nose, and mouth. They were told I was not expected to make it through the night, so my mom did not tell my dad the surgeon's prognosis. She knew repeating that negative report about the severing of my brain from the brainstem could seal my death.

Right after my mom heard these words of the doctors about the severing of the brainstem, she cried out to Jesus for a miracle. She did not repeat the negative report—not even to my dad. She simply began declaring the Word of God over my brainstem area. She declared the life-giving blood of Jesus for the healing of my brain and any damage to the brain- stem. Her faith was strong as she read God's Word over me for my healing.

Three days later, after a CAT scan, when my dad was reunited with my mom and my comatose body, the doctor swung open the door of the hospital room and told my parents he had some news for them. He said with a slightly uplifted tone,

"We did another scan and your son's brain is back on the brain stem." My mom was pretty excited, and excitedly said, "Well does everything look ok where the brain is connected back to the brain stem area?" Looking puzzled at her question, he answered, "It looks fine, but we are puzzled about a fine line where his brain is re-connected to the brain stem. We are uncertain what the fine line is at the brain stem area." At this, my mom raised her voice and said, "Well, I know what the line is! That's where God stitched His brain back to the brainstem!"

CHAPTER 2
LOCKED UP

There is no denying that I was in a coma. The doctors' reports were accurate, but they just did not incorporate the healing power of God that was in process. When I made it through that first night, more negative reports flooded in instead of rejoicing.

They said I was dead at the scene of the accident. They were wrong.
They said I would not live through the night. They were wrong.
They said if I survived, I would be a vegetable. They were wrong.
They said I wouldn't walk again. They were wrong.
They said I would never attend a traditional school again. They were wrong.
They said the only purpose I would ever know would be being confined to a wheelchair in a vegetative, non-functional state. But God said

> *that Jesus came so that I might have life and*
> *have it more abundantly in John 10:10.*
> *They said, they said, they said…*
> *But God said, "Live!"*

My parents had to be on guard constantly to not get caught up in all the negativity. The doctors reported what they thought my condition indicated, according to monitors and tests; it's what doctors do. But my family reported what God said. The doctors were looking at the monitors and machines and did not consider what they could not see with the naked eye. My dad had received a word from God on the plane as he was praying about my condition. God spoke to his heart and told him I would live and not die and declare the works of the Lord.

I know this is the subject of wide debate, but the point is they believed God would heal me and nothing could change what they believed God was doing. They were with me twenty-four/seven, praying and declaring the healing power of Jesus and God's provision for my healing. It was written in His Word! They even took my Bible that was found in the wreckage and read the verses I had underlined in my own Bible. If I had under-lined a verse, the verse meant something to me, and my spirit would recognize the verse. Psalm 107:20 says, "*God sent His Words and healed them and rescued them from their destruction."* These verses from God's Word were healing for my body and food and encouragement for my spirit.

I vividly remember hearing what was being said at times when I was in the coma. I heard my diagnosis. I heard my prognosis. I heard my parents speaking the Word of God directly into my ear. As I heard the Word my parents were speaking, I felt an unexplainable warmth surging through my body. I could feel it moving inside of me.

I *knew* I wasn't dead. Obviously, no one could hear me, but I was aware of their conversations. I was aware of my faith. I was aware of my fears. I was aware of doubt and unbelief. I could actually feel the atmosphere. I knew my family was with me, but I couldn't understand why they wouldn't help me get out of the locked-up place I was in. I remember trying to get everyone's attention. It felt as if I was inside of a glass dome or trapped in a vortex. I knocked and knocked on the glass, trying to get my family's attention — but it wasn't working. I had one other sister, who was not with us in the accident, but was with me almost the entire time I was in the hospital. I could hear my sisters talking, but they were talking about me rather than to me. I felt so frustrated. I was in agony. I was screaming, "Get me out of here!" But my screams were not being heard.

I remember hearing my dad's voice at one point when he walked into my hospital room. I was so excited, thinking, *I know he will help me.* I screamed, "Hey dad, dad, it's me! Help me get out of here!" Of course, he could not hear my screams because I was unable to get sounds through my vocal cords. I felt his hand as he grasped mine. He told me he loved me. However, he wasn't helping me out of my prison. "Dad, dad," I screamed, "get me out of here!" But there was no response to my plea for help.

I remember a moment of consciousness; I am not sure when it was, but we think it was while I was getting a CAT scan during my time at Shands Trauma Center. I remember opening my right eye, but all I saw was the hospital's white walls and nurses in white uniforms walking around.

Being all alone and unable to communicate with anyone was the most horrible feeling. I didn't know where I was; all I knew was my family was not with me. From that one moment, I was plagued with one prevailing thought: *I'm all alone.*

My family was there, all of them, all the time. But that temporary moment of awareness during the CAT scan, with no one I knew anywhere near me, was enough to plant a seed of fear in my heart. At that moment of fear, a stone formed in my heart—a feeling of abandonment. This feeling of being abandoned by my family tormented me.

Where were they, and why did they leave me? As time went on, I even became bitter toward my family for leaving me all alone and not listening to me when I cried out for help.

There are two words that best describe the coma: "locked up." I felt like I was locked up inside my own body. My body was like its own prison, and it was not allowing me to connect with the outside world on any level.

I was trapped inside, silently pleading for someone to hear me and let me out. And, although I felt isolated and alone, the faithful declarations from the Word of God kept me alive as my family read the Word over me day and night. God was sustaining me even when my anger was building against those who loved me.

The hours went by slowly as my family watched and waited for me to come out of the coma. It had been weeks since they'd heard my voice. As I lay there, day after day, without a word, they never gave up hope for my recovery, but continued to declare God's Word over me nearly 24/7.

They brought God's presence into my room. Their faith kept the presence of God so real that it was tangible at times. They would not let a negative report be spoken in my room. They would not let friends or even family members who were wailing and crying come in to see me. They only wanted faith-based words to be expressed in my presence.

My parents were bombarded with so many negative reports. They were told I would not make it through the first night. But I did. They were told that even when the fluid was removed from my brain, the damage was so great that the doctors expected me to be brain dead. Those doctors weren't aware of the healing power of the Word of God and blood of Jesus.

The doctors were just doing their jobs. My parents knew that. They were reporting on what they knew. But, as far as my parents were concerned, they would not entertain any word they received about me that didn't agree with what they were believing from God. It's not that the doctors were intentionally lying to them; it's that they dealt only with what is seen, and not in the unseen truth of God, who was healing my body.

My parents experienced significant pushback from medical professionals when they expressed their faith for my recovery. At one point, a doctor and two nurses came into my room and asked my mom to step outside. They escorted her to a conference room, and told her she was not facing reality. They told her she was in denial about the fact that I was dying, that she needed to calm down, and that she was disrupting the hospital protocol. They suggested she be sedated so she could properly deal with my condition and allow them to carry on. But she refused to be numbed into a stupor.

My mom said she felt alone as she met with the doctor and two nurses and stood up for her faith in God. It was like she was on one side and the entire medical system was on the other. No one believed her that I was being healed. She felt she was a lone soldier in a foreign land with her enemy surrounding her on every side. Neither the doctors nor the nurses were the enemy. The enemy was the system. When a person's vital signs get as low as mine had gotten, certain protocols are activated. These protocols include firing off medical terminology lay persons can't understand. When that happened to my mom, her defense was her shield of faith in God. She made a declaration to defeat her foe. She declared out loud, "I believe in the God of Miracles, and I know He is working a miracle in my son and nothing will stop me from declaring it!"

Nothing could shake my mom or my dad's faith in God. My parents and family were in one accord in the battle for my life. They were all slaying giants. My giants were a paralyzed left side, a coma, and a severe, traumatic brain injury. My parents giants came with every word that tried to convince them that I would not live.

CHAPTER 3

FORTY DAYS IN THE WILDERNESS

On the first two days in the hospital, the doctors did not give my parents any hope of coming out of the coma.

On the third day, I was still alive. The doctors told my family that my carotid artery was clotted and causing strokes. By that time, I had already had multiple strokes. The doctors said with every beat of my heart, the blood that was being pumped to the right side of my brain was accumulating and clotting.

My family was told there was nothing more that could be done. It would just be a matter of time. They were told that my quality of life would be so low that they needed to consider pulling the plug to put me out of my suffering.

When my family heard this report, they began to pray specifically that God would intervene and make His presence known. Suddenly, a different doctor walked in my room and said there was a high-risk surgery he could try. If the procedure was successful, it could stop the clotting. He said if I were his son, he would do the surgery. My parents were convinced the surgeon was sent by God, and they gave him the green light.

There wasn't a moment to lose. Every minute counted. Another stroke could happen at any moment, and the result could be full paralysis or more brain damage.

After the surgery, a couple of hours went by, and the doctor returned to report the procedure had been a success. The clotting had stopped! However, the next hurdle to cross was that my heart needed to beat strong enough to pump blood from the right side of my brain and create a new pathway to the left side of my brain. My parents called for others to join them in this specific prayer. By that time, my heart was weak. I'd suffered from six strokes, but I was still alive!

At this point, my family was being told I would probably live, but that they would have to find a permanent inpatient facility that could manage my recovery from the paralysis. With the severity of my injuries I would be in a vegetable state, and they would not be able to care for me at home.

My family didn't accept that report either. They continued to declare the Word of God and plead the blood of Jesus over me day and night. By this time, a prayer team had come together with prayer warriors from around the world praying for me. At a moment's notice, they would all be activated to pray in one accord about the specific issues that I was facing. The next two weeks were critical, as my temperature spiked and I had to be covered in ice to bring it down. Specific prayer was needed, and within a few hours, my temperature came back to normal. It was touch and go, as I was next diagnosed with pneumonia. With each battle there was a victory, right up to the moment when they began the process of lowering the breathing machine to see if I could breathe on my own.

After twenty-four days in the SHANDS Trauma Center, the doctors told my parents that they had done all they could do for me. I was off the ventilator at this point, but I was still in a coma and unresponsive. The next phase of treatment would be in an inpatient rehabilitation hospital to see if I could gain back movement. The search was on. I was on a feeding tube, so it was hard to find a facility that would take me.

The prayer army was notified, and they began to pray specifically as my parents searched all over the country for a rehabilitation hospital that would take me. The prayers were answered as a bed opened up within four days at Charlotte Rehabilitation Hospital, only an hour from our home.

My high school raised the money to transport me there by medical plane. By this point, I'd been in a coma for twenty-eight days.

Arrangements were made for my dad to fly in the medical plane with me, and my mom would go ahead to get things ready. When she arrived at the rehab hospital ahead of my dad and me, my mom was welcomed by a kind nurse named Ms. Elaine, who told her she had chosen my room and held it until we arrived.

When my dad and I arrived, my mom immediately sensed that something had shifted in me. I couldn't talk, so I couldn't communicate what was happening in my body or in my spirit. But mom knew. She could tell I was barely there. I had taken a plunge in my recovery process. There were no visible signs of this happening, but my mom knew I had digressed. She felt me slipping away. I was giving up.

My mom walked with me from the front entrance of the hospital as the nurse pushed my stretcher down the hall toward my room.

As they walked down the long hall, it was a bleak and dismal sight. Every room they walked by was small and dark, with just the light of a small window. But when they arrived at the end of the hall and opened the door to the room, it was quite a different sight.

My room was a big double room full of light coming through the triple window. My mom, dad, and sisters could see a huge oak tree that was planted right outside the window. It was majestic. The sight of the oak tree was so inspiring to them because it represented thriving life. This tree was a constant reminder that God would raise me up to be a mighty oak of righteousness.

For the next three days, I continued to plummet. My blood pressure dropped, and my vital signs were steadily weakening. At that point, it was critical just to get me back to baseline. While my parents were extremely guarded when I was in the trauma center, once I'd arrived at the rehab hospital, they called in spiritual reinforcements.

They called in God's army; friends and family who were prayer warriors, and upon entering my room, they changed the atmosphere. Their faith became my anchor when I couldn't access my own faith. This was true intercession. I am forever grateful to the warriors who stood in the gap when I couldn't stand for myself.

Even though doctors implied I had very low brain function, I was very much there. I was alive. My eyes were closed, but I could sense what was happening around me.

There seemed to be very little change in my condition, but suddenly, on the thirty-second day,

I finally spoke! I did so in a sedated, monotone, mumbling voice, but what came out was:

"Ezekiel 16:6."

My mom heard it first. She would always sit by my bed in the morning and say to me, "William, let's see what the word of the Lord is today."

Up until that day, when my mom would say this to me, I would always look straight ahead with a blank stare. This particular morning, I said, "Ezekiel 16:6."

"What? What did he just say?" She quickly looked up the scripture. It read:

"And when I passed by you and saw you struggling in your own blood, I said to you in your blood, 'Live!' Yes, I said to you in your blood, 'Live!'"

My mom screamed and danced around the room in celebration that she heard me speak, and even more important was what I spoke. It was a huge breakthrough.

To be clear, I wasn't out of the coma, but I had spoken. It wasn't my brain speaking; it was my spirit. Because I had been so built up in my faith, my spirit spoke before my brain could tell my mouth what to speak. It was a supernatural occurrence, and it was exactly what my family needed to hear: that without a doubt, I would fully recover. They were so convinced, in fact, that they didn't tell any doctors or nurses I had spoken. They knew the supernatural event would have been met with skepticism, doubt, and unbelief. My family refused to open that door for the enemy, so they kept silent.

Just on the other side of my family's stubborn faith—and their relentless commitment to speaking only life over me—was my next major milestone. Around the time I'd said, "Ezekiel 16:6," I opened my eyes and saw that huge oak tree outside my window. I didn't speak about it until years later, but I'd seen it—and it represented the same strength and hope it had represented to my parents. We were in one accord. We all knew God had masterfully orchestrated me having a mighty oak—like His mighty hand—perfectly situated outside my hospital room. The room where I would first speak. The room where hope came alive. The room where my destiny as a living epistle of God's faithfulness would be sealed.

At day forty, things shifted from one dimension to the next. There's something special about the number forty. Throughout the Bible, we see that forty is God's number of transformation and breakthrough. On the fortieth day after the accident, I officially came out of the coma and entered the land of the living. After thirty-nine days of doctors and nurses holding two fingers in front of my face and asking, "William, how many fingers am I holding up?" This time, I responded. I said, "Two." My parents, sisters, and grandparents were all there. They erupted in shouts of joy and praises to God for what He was doing. I also knew my name, I knew how many fingers were waving in front of my face, and I was aware of my surroundings. What had actually happened was, when I said, "Ezekiel 16:6," on the thirty-second day since the accident, I had begun the process of coming out of the coma. After I had supernaturally spoken, it took another eight days for my brain to catch up with the awakening. By day forty, my brain had caught up.

Then, things got real.

I woke up to a physically paralyzed body and a mentally handicapped brain. I couldn't speak fluidly and communicate. I couldn't do anything for myself. In addition to the severe brain injury, I had significant physical limitations due to my paralyzed left side. I couldn't move my left hand, fingers, and arm. My left leg, foot, and toes wouldn't move. I couldn't walk. I wasn't able to move or see out of my left eye, which was locked in a forward-looking position. The left side of my face and mouth was paralyzed, so I couldn't talk or swallow. I also lost half of my hearing on my left side.

The shock of that new reality — and the fact that I'd just awakened from a forty-day coma — was, to say the least, detrimental. I was oblivious to what had happened. I was like an infant who had to learn everything all over again.

During the early days of my recovery, my mother sat beside my bed reading scriptures. She and my dad knew the power of God is released through His Word. All hope of my life having purpose was, as far as I could tell, a distant memory. Visitors came and offered encouragement, but all the people, cards, and emails did little to ease the pain and depression I felt. I was paralyzed. I couldn't move the left side of my body. My left arm, leg, eye, and the left side of my mouth were paralyzed from the six strokes I'd had. These parts of my body were motionless. They were lifeless.

This was a major test. Would I pass or fail? Would I let my circumstances shut me down? Would I give up believing that God — my Healer — is the same yesterday, today, and forever? Would I allow my present circumstances determine my future? It was my test, not my parents'. Like a school exam, I was the only one who could take it and the only one who would pass or fail.

During those endless days and nights when I couldn't talk to people, I talked to my God. I asked Him if I would ever walk again. Day after day, I silently talked with the only One who could hear me. I didn't know if I was passing or failing the test; I just knew I was doing all I could to stay connected to the vine when everything was pulling me to disconnect.

As the days went by and I became more aware of what was going on, the fact that I couldn't walk weighed heavily on me. I was haunted with the fear that I would never walk again. Worse yet, I was afraid I'd never run again. Running was a major part of my life. I had been on the school cross country team and, like many people, I defined who I was through running. Now, my fight started in a conscious state, and my goal was to be able to run again.

CHAPTER 4

ANGELS IN MY ROOM

I believe God divinely placed angels in my room—or at the very least, people with an anointing, incredibly tailored specific to my needs—to minister to me. Hebrews 13:2 encourages us to always be mindful that we could be entertaining angels. If the people He sent weren't angels, they were extremely obedient vessels who were clearly receiving a word from God about me. There's a saying, "Whether you believe it or not, it is so." There's no doubt in my mind that angels are real.

The first angel I want to share about is my special nurse, Ms. Elaine. She was a helper for me and all my family to fight this battle. When we first arrived in the Charlotte Rehab, she was the one who escorted us to my room. She said, "I've been waiting on y'all. The Lord told me to save this room, and I didn't let anybody else get it." Ms. Elaine was a wonderful nurse; she would rub my paralyzed arm and say, "Mister William, Mister

William, the Lord loves you, Mister William. The Lord is healing you, Mister William." She ministered to me by calling out my name over and over.

In talking with Ms. Elaine, my family found out she had ministered to many famous people like Billy Graham, both President George Bush and his father, as well as other well-known pastors, leaders, and evangelists. She was an older lady who had a lot of experience ministering to people with strokes and brain injuries. She taught us many things that most people probably don't know. Every morning she would come into my hospital room, throw my covers back, and put my tennis shoes on me. Then she would say, "Ok, Mister William, let's get going." This seemed odd to me because I could not move my legs or walk. Through this action, she was preparing and declaring that I would walk again. She took prophetic action and put my shoes on every day, as if she was fully expecting me to walk that day. As she put on my sneakers for the first time, she dumped out all the broken glass that remained from the accident, but she didn't let it move her. Ms. Elaine hoisted my paralyzed body into a wheelchair, strapped me in, stabilized my bobbing head, and whisked me around the facility as if I would jump out of that chair at any moment.

One of my fond memories is of Ms. Elaine pushing me fast down the hall. I hated the wheelchair, but she made a game of it. When I could push myself in the wheelchair, we would race down the hall. As I reflect on the thought of Ms. Elaine chasing me down the hall in the wheelchair, it is a profound memory that brings me a lot of joy.

Ms. Elaine knew that my heart's desire was to walk out of Charlotte Rehab, and she helped me accomplish that. We talked about the day I would walk out. She didn't remind me of what I couldn't do; she told me I could and would indeed walk again! Ms. Elaine treated me as if I could already talk, walk, and function normally. She refused to talk down to me, pity me, or relate to me in my debilitated state. She related to me as a vibrant, healed, whole, young man. Every day, she would come into my room and say, "Okay, Mister William, we're going outside today." Ms. Elaine was the constant voice telling me I would walk again. She refused to believe otherwise.

My mom told me of another visitor who came into my room every night around midnight. This visitor was a janitor who would come in and pray for me. He would not turn the light on; he would sweep, dust, and mop as he softly prayed. My mom could hear him saying, "Mister William, I'm praying for you," then again, "Mister William, I'm praying for you." Just like Ms. Elaine, no one knew anything about him when we went back to see everyone a year later. It was as if Ms. Elaine and the janitor did not even exist in the hospital system's payroll, but we knew they were paid well because they were on God's payroll.

During my time in the hospital, there were many occasions where I could see the hand of God moving. Both in the people of faith that God brought into the hospital room to minister to my family and I, and in the divine healing miracles that took place in my body, it was obvious that God was always moving. As my family read and prayed the Word of God over me in faith, I believe that God honored and answered their prayers. Whether through the healing that happened in my body, or through the angels or divinely placed individuals, God was always on the move.

On another occasion, there was a kind nurse who came to my room just once. This nurse was dressed in white with blonde hair; she was radiantly beautiful. She stood on the side of my bed and asked my mom, "What music does your son like? You know, being a teenager, do you know what his favorite group is?" My mom replied that I liked the Christian group called Third Day. She then reached into her pocket and pulled out a Third Day CD! It was as if that was her only assignment because we never saw her again.

After I got out of the hospital, I saw the CD and asked where it came from, and my mom told me the story about the mystery nurse who brought it. The interesting thing was that the CD had all my favorite songs on it. We have no doubt that God sends His angels as ministering servants, just like the Bible says.

My parents told me that after I had been in the hospital a few days, God performed a miracle that was visible. While my pastor's wife was sitting with my parents, she left them for a minute to visit me. She looked at my face and noticed something had happened to my front tooth. It wasn't sticking out anymore, as she had seen it earlier that morning. She ran out of the room to get everyone. She couldn't believe her eyes. She screamed, "You have to come see what's happened!" After the accident, my front tooth that had been straightened by braces was sticking straight out. The tooth was lying on one of the largest tubes going into my mouth and down my throat. When they all ran into my room they saw it—my tooth had moved, and it was completely straight again. The tubes had not been moved; they were still tightly wedged into my mouth. They asked the nurse on duty, if she was aware of anything that had occurred that could have shifted my tooth, but she had not been in the room. but she had not been in the room. God had moved my tooth back to its previous position and had begun the process of manifesting Revelation 21:5—making all things new.

CHAPTER 5

THE POWER OF WORDS

Words are powerful. They create things. They change circumstances. They are full of life or full of death. I believe the words spoken over and into me are responsible for me being alive today.

Proverbs 18:21 says, *"Death and life are in the power of the tongue, and those who love it will eat its fruit."*

People can either speak positive, empowering words that are life to you, or speak negative, critical words that can deaden your spirit and cause sorrow and depression. I would not be where I am today without the positive influence of motivating, encouraging mentors in my life.

I remember my pastor Jeff Rowland's words to me early on, when I was in rehab. He looked down at me in my wheelchair and said, "Man, you're looking strong." Those words landed directly in my spirit. By speaking strength to me, he showed me he truly cared. I felt significant and had a renewed hope. My pastor also said, "William, you *will* walk again. It's in your name! The great 'I Am' is in your name." After he told me about the meaning of my name, he spoke a blessing over me and prayed for me. Those encouraging words from my pastor were one of the main motivators that kept me pressing forward. They were the foundation for me to get out of that wheelchair. I always had his encouraging words in the back of my mind when I walked with a walker across the therapy room. I can't begin to explain to you how hearing those words motivated me to not only walk, but run again. I kept telling myself that I would run again. Pastor Jeff's words were not his own; he was just the messenger God used to bring me the message. The thought of possibly not being able to run did cross my mind a few times, but I had gained so much hope from Pastor Jeff's words. When someone declares life over you, it is amazing how that can push you through doubts so that you can believe in yourself. I did struggle with doubts and discouragement; however, each time I was tempted with even the hint to give up, I forced myself to remember Pastor Jeff's words.

My mom quoted Bible verses like David's words in Psalms, *"I will run through a troop and leap over a wall" (Psalm 18:29).* At the time, I knew I felt encouraged, but I didn't realize how powerful an effect those words were having on my life until much later.

The old saying goes, "Sticks and stones may break my bones, but words will never hurt me." Satan must have made that one up, because it's a flat out lie. It's literally the opposite of what the Bible teaches. Proverbs 18:21 says that words can kill you or breathe life into you. If my pastor would have spoken negative words instead of positive ones, I would have believed them, and I would have lived them. My life would have played out exactly as those words were spoken. My pastor only spoke life over and into me, but I can't underscore enough how critical it was that I only heard God's Word and confirmations of His promises about my future.

My parents only allowed people they knew would speak life-giving and encouraging words to visit me. This was a major undertaking. It was warfare! That meant my parents had to say "no" to a lot of well-meaning people, and a lot of feelings got hurt. My parents couldn't worry about that, though. My life was at stake, and they couldn't risk my life on the words of well-meaning people who didn't know how to talk the way God talks. This is a kingdom principle, and people often get offended when it's applied correctly. My parents did exactly what Jesus did because they understood the power of words.

"Get out!" Jesus told them. "The girl isn't dead; she's only asleep." But the crowd laughed at him. After the crowd was put outside, however, Jesus went in and took the girl by the hand, and she stood up!"
(Matthew 9:24-25) (NLT).

If it was necessary for Jesus to remove doubting people for healing to take place, it was necessary for my parents to follow the same example so that I would obtain my healing.

Throughout the initial recovery process, my family and I were barraged with negative statements that did not align to God's truth. The doctors said, *"Your son is going to have to go to an institutionalized school."*

We have to be mindful of words that are spoken over us that can cause fear. Since my parents had refused to put me in a permanent inpatient facility and informed the doctors they would provide my care, the doctors told them that if they did not significantly intensify my physical therapy, I would be in a wheelchair for the rest of my life. Thoughts came to my head, like, *I won't have a normal life again*, and, *I'll never have friends again*. I admit, more than once, I gave in and believed I would never walk or run again. Keep in mind, I was fifteen years old. I was already at an awkward age.

Having to process the kind of trauma I had experienced was a brand-new ball game for me.

During the early days of my recovery, my mother sat beside me all day, reading scriptures over me. She knew the power of God is released through His Word. That is why I had faith to battle the lies. The Word had built up my faith. As my mom read the Word over me, I could feel something moving inside my paralyzed body—a heat deep inside me. The soothing heat covered me like a blanket on a cold night. I don't recall all the specific scriptures she was reading; I just recall the warmth as she spoke the Word over me. I knew the words were from God.

Life-giving words gave me the motivation to tell my physical therapist that I wanted to walk out of rehab without assistance. She said, "Okay, you can do it, but we're going to have to work extra hard if you really want to walk out of here without a cane or walker." That was all I needed to hear. I worked so hard and talked, often in broken sentences, about how I would walk out of the hospital. I set a goal to walk out of that rehab hospital. I was determined to reach that goal. Setting goals was a good way to battle my fears. Words were a major factor in my victory, and they are a major factor in my current daily life.

James 3:4-6 says,
Indeed, we put bits in horses' mouths that
they may obey us, and we turn their whole
body. Look also at ships: although they are
so large and are driven by fierce winds, they
are turned by a very small rudder wherever
the pilot desires. Even so the tongue is a little
member and boasts great things. See how great
a forest a little fire kindles! And the tongue is
a fire, a world of iniquity. The tongue is so set
among our members that it defiles the whole
body and sets on fire the course of nature; and
it is set on fire by hell.

All my achievements were the result of the Word of God spoken over my circumstances.

You may never realize how your uplifting or encouraging words can positively influence someone, but they can. Many of the words I have heard over the years have inspired me because they were spoken *from* a spirit of truth and power. Likewise, the negative words I heard caused me to struggle. Therefore, it is so important for anyone with any kind of unfavorable medical diagnosis — and even those who aren't battling any kind of sickness — to very closely monitor the friends and acquaintances you allow in your life. Whether you realize it or not, everyone in your life is influencing you in some way. Everyone in your life is speaking either God's language or the enemy's language. You can choose either a group of life talkers or death talkers.

God gave my mom a verse on the third day after my accident. The verse was Revelation 21:5: "… behold I make all this new." The word "behold" in this verse means to see something with your own eyes. God was going to allow my family to see with their own eyes that He was making everything in my body new, starting with my tooth.

Family and friends all over the country — and all over the world — had been praying for me day and night. Every single moment of the day, God's Word was being declared over me. From the straightened tooth to my feet walking, every single evidence of progress was God accomplishing Revelation 21:5. It was such a clear indication of the power of prayer and positive declarations.

CHAPTER 6
THE WILL OF GOD

M y name has purpose in it. The very word "will" (the core of my formal name, William) has been — and remains — the driving force of my life. I had to have the "will" not to give up and be overcome by my circumstances. Rather than having an "I'll try" attitude, I had to have an "I will" attitude. The Will of God was for me to live and not die, to thrive and not just survive. I can see now that my Unshakable Destiny was the will of God, but I had to buy into it and pursue it with every fiber of my being.

A full understanding of my name came as I sat mute in a wheelchair. When my pastor said, "William, your name is WILL-I-AM. You have the 'Will' to walk, and the Great I AM is going to help you walk again!" Those words resonated with me. From that moment on, I chose to live — to walk and talk again and declare hope of a new life to other people. I made a decision: *I am "Will" and the great "I AM" is inside me. I can't lose for winning.*

My purpose was inside of me all the time because Christ in me is the hope of glory.

In biblical times, a man's name revealed his purpose in life. I thought I would find my purpose in another man's book. The irony of course is my (and your) purpose is found in a book—not any book, but the Holy Bible.

Looking back, I don't think I would have understood that principle without walking through it first. As a fifteen-year-old, I couldn't fathom that my purpose was in my name. God laid out the path I had to walk to discover my purpose. God used the horrifying accident, which nearly took my life, to lead me down a path that would simultaneously test me and reveal my purpose and mirror His glory for many people. In my case, I came to truly know the Great I Am—the One who is the giver of life—through a near-death experience. This won't be everyone's experience, but the principle of discovering purpose can be universally applied through my story.

Through it all, I learned one simple truth: God said I would live, and that indicated I had a purpose to fulfill. Because He said I would live, my family believed that He was perfectly capable of restoring me and that He's not just a promise maker; He's a promise keeper. God expected my family and me to believe I would survive the coma and recover to proclaim His goodness and healing power. God promised salvation, life, and healing, but my parents had to cooperate with Him. It was up to my parents and me to think, speak, and act in a way that positioned us to *receive* those promises and walk in the fullness of them. It took a while, but eventually, I had hope that God had more planned for me than being confined to a wheel-chair for the rest of my life—and I believed it!

CHAPTER 7

IN PREPARATION FOR MY JOURNEY

Preparation for the journey that would reveal my Unshakable Destiny started with my passion to find my purpose. I had thought reading *The Purpose Driven Life* was the only thing that would help me find my purpose. But learning to trust Jesus Christ, and not becoming bitter in the most difficult time of my life was the preparation for finding my purpose.

God has a purpose for our lives. He has created everyone, without exception, with His purpose downloaded deep in their spirit.

While I never would have anticipated — or wanted — to be in a car accident, I did know God had not changed His mind about my purpose. He would somehow turn around what the enemy meant for evil for my good. I clung to that truth. I couldn't view the challenges that came with my recovery as misfortunes, but rather I had to embrace them as part of my training for my purpose.

Keep in mind, I said God turns what the enemy means for evil around for our good. This is far different from God creating problems in our lives. God is not and never will be responsible for sending problems into our lives for the mere enjoyment of seeing us suffer. He is a good Father. He allows problems to mold and shape us to become better, more devoted Christ-followers.

That day of the accident, a series of events unfolded which turned out to be far different from what I expected as a purpose. As I reflect on my words, "Hey Mom, how about if I just read *The Purpose Driven Life* straight through over spring break?" I realize that in the moments following those words, God accelerated the journey of purpose He had for me. I would soon encounter one of the worst events of my life. Despite the fiery trial I was about to face, God's hand was carrying me the whole way through, protecting, molding, and shaping me into the man He had planned for me to become. The trials we face in life may seem unbearable, but if we continue to trust in God, He will see us through and mold us into the person He wants us to be.

As a cross country runner, I could readily relate to having a glimpse of the finish line. I wanted to see what my life was going to look like, but I thought all I needed to do was read a book with the word "purpose" in the title. I didn't realize God's plans for me would be revealed experientially.

I cannot stress more how God sent incredibly gifted, anointed vessels to help me through my journey of recovery. My first physical therapist was Shanna. At first, I thought she seemed mean, but she wasn't. She was just determined to see me walk. She had to be strong to push me out of paralysis. She was the one who would make me put weights on my weak, skinny legs. I had lost so much weight that I was just a bunch of bones wrapped in skin. She harnessed me up in a contraption that held me in the air, then she turned a crank that lowered me down until my legs touched the ground.

As she lowered me a little at a time, it felt like my right leg was going to snap, and I couldn't feel the left one at all. My arms were dangling, and my head was bobbing. I can't imagine what it was like for my parents, who had seen me run seven miles a day, to see me not being able to stand up by myself. My body was so weak from laying in a bed for so long that I could only stand on my legs for a few minutes in the harness.

Each day being in the harness was pressing me to put a little more weight on my legs. While the harness helped me stand on my legs, I was forcing myself to spiritually stand again. Just as

God's purpose was for me to walk again, His plan for my life had not changed, considering my current situation.

As my determination was tested, my faith was as fragile as my legs. The Bible is full of examples of great men and women of God whose purpose was tested. While I was being strapped into the harness each day, I had to remember Moses. He was tested multiple times before he was ready to lead the children of Israel out of Egypt. As He did with Moses, God required me to trust Him enough with the challenge I was facing. It's interesting that Moses was on the backside of the desert for forty years preparing for his purpose, and I was in a coma for forty days preparing for mine. God does not allow us to see our full purpose all at once. If He did, we wouldn't go through with it. Instead, He directs us one step at a time.

I didn't know it would be such a long journey, and I'm sure Moses probably didn't either. When God told him to lead the people to the Promised Land, Moses had a glimpse of the finish line. I believe the glimpse of the Promised Land God gave him kept Moses going through those hard years in the wilderness.

CHAPTER 8

PRESSING IN!

Day after day, I would look down at my paralyzed legs in the wheelchair, visualizing them running again, but they were not moving. My thoughts were in conflict. I began to be double-minded. On one hand, I saw, with my spiritual eyes, my legs running. On the other hand, I thought it would take a lifetime to walk again. My mind was divided, and I didn't know what to believe. I had to learn that seeing is not believing; believing is how we will see what we are hoping for.

During those early days of inpatient rehab, I was constantly wondering if I would experience a full life again, considering all of the negative reports. At some point, I heard the doctors say, "This is all he is going to progress." My parents have told me the doctors tried to convince them they needed to put me in an institution specifically for people with such a severe condition as myself.

I was angry at my circumstances, angry at my legs for not moving, and angry that there was nothing I could do about it. At one point during therapy, I was so angry that when I tried to lift myself out of the wheelchair, I would repeatedly fall on my face. Feeling defeated, I had to face my own enemies. I faced the fear of being trapped in a disabled, paralyzed body, in a wheelchair the rest of my life. I faced the fear of not being able to go on with my education and the fear of facing my peers.

With each day I sat in the wheelchair, I looked down the dismal hospital walls with sorrow as I saw all the people in wheelchairs. I believe now that if I had been put in an institution, I would still be in that wheelchair. I would have learned to adapt and give in to that environment.

My cognitive abilities were negatively impacted too. I remember hearing one psychiatrist tell my mom I was at a third-grade level of comprehension and would not be able to go back to my high school. She said I would have to go to a special needs school. I heard these devastating words and halfway believed them, but something inside of me kept me believing that if Jesus had spared my life from the accident, then He was going to continue to heal me.

The first movement on my paralyzed left side was my little pinky finger. My mom would say over and over, "Will, tell your brain to move your finger." I would hear her say that and think hard, "Fingers, move." But nothing happened.

We did this over and over, and then one day, it happened—my pinky finger moved. My mom jumped out of her chair, screaming, "He moved it! He moved his pinky finger!" But it was a hollow victory for me. I couldn't make my other fingers do what I wanted them to do. It almost felt like my hand and fingers were held together by glue. When I think back on it now, the Lord wanted me to be thankful and celebrate the small progress, and then I would experience more. Surely enough, as time passed, the other fingers began to move, one after the other. Persevering and not giving up paid off. After I learned to move my fingers, I learned to lift my entire arm. We take small movements for granted until we lose them.

My mom and sisters would take me to the workout room and throw balls at me. My mom reminded me that when she first started this exercise, I just sat there in the wheelchair with a blank stare on my face. But later, I had progressed to moving my arm to catch the ball. By now, the whole family had gotten involved. I would make a slight movement of my arm and everyone would cheer. My family were my greatest cheerleaders as they kept pushing me and cheering me on. Every tiny movement was celebrated, and that encouraged me to press on. There were many obstacles while I was fighting to break free from my paralyzed body.

I was still confined to a wheelchair, completely dependent on others to get me where I needed to go. Humbling myself in this way and allowing other people to do things I had always done for myself was another test I had to pass. My purpose required it. I remember when my uncles Don and Tommy and Aunt Martha came to visit. Uncle Don stood on one side and Uncle Tommy on the other. One would shovel in a mouthful of food, and then the other would shovel in the next bite. If that doesn't press you to get out of the paralyzed state and feed yourself, I don't know what else will.

As my fingers were moving, I was also gaining more movement in my mouth and vocal cords to sound out simple sentences. One victory of movement gave me the faith to keep pressing toward the next one. When I got discouraged, my mom would remind me to tell my brain what I wanted my fingers and arms to do. My brain was being retrained in how to communicate with the sleeping side of my body.

I was communicating more and more each day, which was exciting but at the same time puzzling for some of the therapists. With the severity of my injuries, I was surpassing all by the progress I was making.

The next challenge was learning to feed myself. When you are learning everything all over again, it's clumsy and awkward at first. I would drop the food off my fork right before I got it to my mouth. I had daily struggles, but again, I was very determined.

I admit, sometimes I wanted to quit. I think if I had been left to myself, I would have given up many times. I needed every family member — each of my grandparents; both my parents; my sisters, Casey and Crystal; and my brother in law, Jon. Even my aunts and uncles had a part. It took my whole family pushing me. My family frequently used the expression, "Press in; you got to press in," which means go as deep as God requires you to manifest the result He's promised.

God said I would live. He didn't say I would live handicapped. He didn't say I would live disabled. He said I would live abundantly (John 10:10). But, at this point in the process, pressing in seemed too hard. My whole world had stopped, and I couldn't see beyond the wheelchair. So what if I couldn't feed myself? So what if I would be stuck in a wheelchair the rest of my life? But, by the grace of God, the root of my name — Will — wouldn't let quitting be an option. The Word of God spoken over me to live would not return to Him void.

I believe God's purpose for our lives extends through our lifetime. Circumstances that disagree with God's plans are irrelevant. We must not allow our circumstances to speak louder than our Savior. If we listen to our circumstances, we can allow them to shut us down and rob us of our belief in God's purpose. We must believe that the One who created us will see to it that His purpose is carried out; this is why, if we believe, we can have an Unshakable Destiny. Our purpose is what makes us press through and experience a full and meaningful life.

When we can look at what we're going through and realize God is using it for our good, there's a different motivation to press in. God becomes bigger than the thing we're going through.

I realized I had a choice: life or death (Prov. 18:21). If I looked at my legs and my self-talk said, *I'll never get out of this wheelchair*, I would be stuck there. If I had stayed in despair, depression, and bitterness, I would still be in a wheelchair today. But, when I chose to look at my paralyzed legs with hope, I gained motivation to press in and make my therapy work as an act of faith.

Another test I had to pass was overcoming bitterness. This was a big one!

As Jesus hung on the cross, the Roman soldiers offered Him vinegar, which was considered the most bitter of all beverages. He refused it. The enemy offered me bitterness in the form of the word "why." Why did I have to endure the pain of this accident and the painful process of becoming whole again?

The injustice of it weighed on me. Why was I unable to read now when I was once an "A" student? Why was I unable to walk when I was once a cross country runner? Why?

I had a choice. I could either be bitter or press in with Christ and be better. To choose Christ and press in was a daily choice. I'll say that again; it bears repeating. I had to intentionally make a choice — every day — to let my spirit, rather than my flesh, tell me what to do, how to think, and what to say. In time, it was this daily choice that helped me realize that the injuries I sustained would be used for His glory.

I am gifted now to minister to those who have experienced a traumatic or hopeless event, including a TBI (Traumatic Brain Injury). As I progressed in my recovery, I began to understand that my injuries enabled me to have compassion to minister to hopeless, hurting people, including those who may have had a TBI, a group of people to whom I would have never otherwise related. God has given me a special burden to minister to any kind of hopeless or hurting person.

God can use anything we go through for His glory. If I had held on to bitterness, my ministry to people in hopeless situations would have been completely derailed.

What if the difficult situation you are facing right now is preparation for your purpose tomorrow? Will you press in and pass each test? Believe me, it's worth it.

CHAPTER 9

THE ANTAGONIST

Learning how to pass through physical and emotional difficulties — without getting stuck — is the key to overcoming self-pity.

After looking down at my weak legs and feeling sorry for myself, I can say that I know what being stuck feels like. I would smile at friends who would come visit me in the hospital, but I couldn't carry on a conversation with them, much less get up out of the bed and go to school the next day. When they left my room, my uninvited friend, self-pity, and I would talk about how bad I had it.

Then, when I was in cognitive therapy and couldn't see the letters on the screen that were enlarged as large as they could go, I would get another visit from self-pity.

One of my worst days was when a speech therapist came in my room talking to me like a first-grader and offered me a cherry sucker. "Lady, I am not a first-grader, and I hate cherry suckers!" But, as with so many others, she couldn't hear my screams. I was stuck; I couldn't communicate, and I felt sorry for myself.

During those hard days of feeling handicapped, incompetent, and depressed, there would always be a way of escape—a loving person, a kind word, or an encouraging smile that gave me a glimmer of hope that God had not forgotten me.

The visits from my family members, such as Nana and Papa, were especially encouraging, as well as those from high school friends and teachers that visited me. All these gave me hope that I was not alone in this battle to recover.

A young man named Peter and a couple others from Fire Ministry School in Charlotte came to visit and pray for me. I felt so special that they would take time to visit someone they didn't even know. Peter let me strum his guitar a little bit, and then he sang a song. That was pretty much the highlight of my whole month. It meant so much to me that those ministry students cared enough to come visit me, a teenager who was paralyzed and could hardly talk.

I learned that self-pity was not a friend to listen to, but an antagonist I had to resist daily. If I let my mind wander and think about why the accident had happened to me, self-pity would return. Once I started changing my thought process, I saw less and less of self-pity. From that day forward, I began meditating on the positive things, like what I had accomplished in therapy that day.

I vividly remember that day—the day I finally overcame. As I sat on my bed in the rehab hospital, I looked out the window at that majestic oak tree. I cried out to God, "If You can make that tree grow and thrive so everyone can see it, God, I ask You to raise me up out of this bed and make me like that mighty oak. I want out of here. I know I have an assignment beyond these four walls. I want to be free from self-pity, so I can be who You created me to be." This may seem like a simple prayer, but I know it reached heaven; I felt different from that day on! I would not listen to self-pity again. From the day I prayed to be set free from the antagonist, I felt the power of God surging inside of me more than ever! I could feel it moving me in a different direction.

If I had listened to the voice of self-pity, I would not have been able to move forward toward God's purpose for me.

We all face difficulties, but we can overcome them if we choose to listen only to God and move toward Him, never give up, and wait on God's timing. Waiting does not mean sitting around doing nothing. We pray and wait, like a waiter in a restaurant. During the waiting time, as I was building up my strength to resist the enemy, I needed to keep my mind on what God had promised me and not give up.

As I was waiting on God, every moment, I was filling my mind with the truth. An idle mind will set you up to listen to the lies of the enemy, and his goal is to convince you to give up. My family had to wait forty days for me to wake up from the coma, and they never gave up. You might say I was fighting on the inside to come out of the coma and my family was fighting on the outside to pull me out. We were never idle.

Waiting on God did not mean my parents were sitting around watching TV. Waiting on God meant they had to believe God was working, and their part was to be on guard and not let anyone sabotage what God was doing. While you're waiting on God, you don't allow yourself to give up or give in. My parents did not allow anyone who had a negative attitude or didn't believe in healing to come into my room. They were on guard! As they were waiting on my movements, they were declaring the Word over me and playing worship music in my room to create an atmosphere of faith.

Let's be honest. No one *likes* to wait on God. We tend to want to give up and let up when things don't suit our timing. I progressed, but that progression was slow. My healing certainly wasn't happening in my timing. Remember, I'm the guy who wanted to figure out my life's purpose over spring break.

The accident did not take my purpose away from me. God used what the enemy meant to steal, kill, and destroy to produce in me the realization that I had to grab hold of His plans for my life. That alone was what enabled me to persevere and overcome the obstacles I faced.

CHAPTER 10

PASSING THE THRESHOLD

The day came to take my first step. The very first step I took with the walker wore me out, and I fell backwards into my chair. My legs were so weak that they could not hold up my body without folding up under me.

I admit, I would get angry at myself and wanted to give up, but that first step was a major milestone; my family all celebrated each time I took an additional step. I remember my Aunt Martha, Uncle Tommy, and Uncle Don were there to see it. They were so proud of me, and my Aunt Martha screamed and cried. The support from my family kept me pressing on as they cheered me on with every step.

I went from taking my first few steps with the walker to ten steps down the hall. Ms. Elaine was always close behind with the wheelchair if I ever got too tired.

As I progressed more and more with getting out of the wheelchair, feeding myself, tying my shoes, and pulling my shirt over my head, the nurse told me it was time to begin preparing to go home. I even had to learn how to get in and out of the car.

I was beyond excited when the day for me to go home finally arrived. I had practiced loading myself into a vehicle for transport. I had even practiced using handicap ramps and shower stools so I could bathe myself. I was ready to go!

Then the moment I had been waiting for arrived, and I was determined I would walk out of that hospital. Yes! I had determined I would walk out through the threshold. I had come in on a stretcher, and I was going out on my own two legs. Yes, my own two legs, not with a walker. Everyone was there! The hospital staff had nicknamed me "The Miracle Boy," so it was a big deal when the day came for me to leave the hospital. Ms. Elaine and I had it all planned out. She pushed me to the front door and helped me stand up. Then, to everyone's surprise, she held on to me as I walked out the door. Yes, I walked across the threshold of the front door.

God had heard my cry to be able to walk out of the hospital, and He sent an angel to make sure it was accomplished. As I stepped over the threshold, and took three more steps to load myself into our car, I knew for sure Ms. Elaine was an angel.

Even though I couldn't express to anyone how I felt about Ms. Elaine, I really connected with her and drew strength from her. I knew in my heart God had sent her specifically to help me walk again.

CHAPTER 11

I WILL RUN AGAIN!

Runners think about crossing the finish line. They rehearse the race over and over in their minds. They have a glimpse of what it will be like to cross the finish line, and they can even hear the sound of the cheering crowd. Everyone cheered me on as I crossed the finish line of the Charlotte Rehabilitation Hospital. Being confined to a wheelchair was one of my greatest fears, and I asked God to give me a peek of what it would be like to walk out of that rehab hospital.

But that was just the first finish line I would cross. There would be many more, all of which came after races with different routes, lengths, peaks, valleys, obstacles, and levels of difficulty.

As my dad loaded the wheelchair into the trunk of the car that day, I was determined I would not have to use that wheelchair again. I quietly said, "That chair will not hold me back. I will walk, and with God's help, I will run cross country again." I believed with everything in my being that I would run again.

As we approached my home, the road was lined with yellow balloons. In front of my house was a big "Welcome Home" banner. My grandparents, Nana and Papa, were there, and Nana had baked my favorite chocolate chip cookies. All my school friends, teachers, and other friends were crowded around the huge banner. It was a day I will never forget.

When I got home, I faced a different world. The obstacles in front of me were on a much higher level. It was like jumping from kindergarten to high school. In the back of my mind, I was thinking that when I got home, my life would return to the "normal" I once knew. The young man I was before the accident was still inside me, and I thought he would come back. But he didn't come back right away.

My family worked with me almost non-stop—all day, every day, helping me learn how to do everything all over again. All we did was therapy. Just sitting down for dinner was all about therapy—using a fork, using a napkin, picking up my glass of tea. I had to learn not to reach and grab my food with my fingers or the food on the plate of whoever was sitting beside me. Every activity seemed to turn into therapy to press me forward in my recovery. In some ways, it was like waking up from a long dream and trying to figure out why life had changed while I was asleep.

My speech, motor skills, and walking continued to improve. It had been six months since I had arrived home from the rehab hospital, and I still couldn't run. I was determined not to give up. I continued to improve with walking until, one day while practicing, I picked up a little speed and power walked down the hall. That was my first marathon!

Over time, I increased to a slow, unstable jog so that I was able to get down the hall faster. Excitedly, I told my physical therapist, Dr. Drew, that I had run or walked fast down the hallway, and I wanted to work on perfecting my run.

Then I tried running down the hall. I don't mean a smooth run; I mean a stumbling, falling, hitting-the-sides-of-the-walls run. But it didn't stop me. I was determined to practice inside until I was able to gain enough strength to go outside.

I repeated over and over in my mind, *My name is William, and I "will" run again because God, the Great I Am, is inside of me.*

One day, I had a preview of the next finish line: I saw myself running in the field behind our house. Could I graduate from awkwardly running down the hall to running in a rocky, unstable field?

Yes, I Will!

My running slowly improved. I went to regular outpatient physical therapy appointments to work on my walking and to strengthen my legs to try to work on my running. I finally graduated from the hall to the backyard. My family continued to cheer me on. They worked with me and encouraged me to keep going. They agreed with me in believing God was rebuilding the strength in my legs so I could run in the field.

The day before the accident, I ran seven miles. So, it became my goal to run cross country again. At that moment, that was my ultimate goal, my ultimate finish line.

After a year (yes, a full year) of very intense physical therapy and training, I graduated from the backyard to the field behind our house. I came in beat up and bleeding from so many falls, but it didn't bother me. I was determined to get back on the cross country team.

CHAPTER 12
BACK TO SCHOOL

E valuation after evaluation, the cognitive ther-apist told my parents I would not be able to go back to my high school. They endlessly tested me, even up to the day before I went home from the rehab hospital. Each test result revealed that my understanding was at a first- or second-grade level. This was incredibly difficult for me to accept. I had enough memory to recall that I had been in high school and was a straight-A student.

The thought of *not* being able to go back to my high school terrified me. The thought of having to go to a school as a handicapped person haunted me. The doctors and psychiatrists warned my family that I would not be able to handle a normal high school environment. But with God, all things are possible! In the fall of 2005, I was able to return to my Christian school. I started as a sophomore and ended up graduating with my class with honors. My doctor later told me that this was med-ically impossible, considering that so many brain cells had been destroyed. But with God, all things are possible!

Because of God's miraculous power, I was recovering far beyond what they had expected, but I was still in a handicapped condition.

After constantly training my brain all summer, I gained abilities the doctors had said I would never have again. We came up with a phrase called "retraining my brain." Everything I had lost had to be retrained—everything from tying my shoe to brushing my teeth. My brain could be retrained because my parents had refused the medications that the rehab hospital doctors prescribed for me. This was medication given to Alzheimer's patients, and it would have slowed down my brain function so that it wouldn't have been able to be retrained.

To retrain my brain, my entire family had to get involved. I had to relearn everything I had learned in my first fifteen years of life, from the simplest to the most complex task. But before the task could be trained, my brain had to learn through repetition how to do simple things. One of the most beneficial therapies I did over and over was working puzzles. I would look at the picture on the box and then turn it over and try to recall the picture as I put the pieces together. To show you how impaired I was, my first puzzle was four blocks that a one-year-old learns how to turn a certain way to make a picture. I progressed from four pieces to a board puzzle of twenty large pieces that four- and five-year-olds can easily work. Then I progressed to the box puzzles.

Another therapy my parents came up with to retrain my brain was showing me family pictures to work on my memory. They would ask me questions of where we were and what we were doing at the time each picture was taken. I prayed and asked God to help me learn and to accelerate my learning ability. He heard my petition. So many brain cells had been destroyed that one section of my brain was black on the CAT scan. Again, this shows the magnitude of my healing. My family doctor, Dr. Sam Stout, would just look at me every time I went for a check-up and say I was absolutely a walking miracle.

Worship has always been a part of my life. My parents played worship music in my hospital room twenty-four/seven—the entire time. I continued having the same worship music playing in my room for several years after the accident. Worship music is healing to the brain. I needed the brain cells I had lost to be replenished, and the worship music helped to turn off my thoughts so my mind could rest. I truly believe that God used the worship music to replenish my lost brain cells.

As soon as I could see again, I began to look at pictures in magazines and connect the words with the pictures. Then I began to try reading books. At first, it was the large print books that children read, and as I improved, the reading became easier. If I was going to be able to go back to school in the fall, I knew I had to learn to read again. It was like I started first grade all over again. I read all summer and progressed until I got to my grade level of reading.

When the day for school to start back finally arrived, I wanted so badly to just be a normal teenager again. I wanted to walk like a normal kid and go back to school and hang out with all my friends. But that time was over; I had to face my new reality. Nothing would ever be the same for me at school. I had to face the loss of my life as it once was and embrace my new normal. I was afraid, to say the least. I was afraid all my friends would all see me walking with a cane, or stumbling down the hall, and refuse to talk to me. Unfortunately, many of these fears came to pass. The people who had once been my friends simply did not know how to react to me. I was not the same Will that left for spring break, and they didn't know what to do with the new Will.

My biggest challenge with returning to school was interacting with my peers. After a few weeks back at school, I realized that I had lost most of my friends. The only way they knew how to relate to me was by making fun of me. I became their source of comic relief. They poked at me, tripped me, and made jokes about my disabilities. For someone with a brain injury, losing friends can be a crippling blow that makes it hard to reach out and make new friends. Even if I made a new friend, because of all my fears, it was extremely hard to keep them. My true friends were selfless, and they were few and far between. In fact, most of them didn't go to my high school.

After I returned to school, two events occurred that forever changed me, as well as the lives of the students in my small Christian school. At the end of my sophomore year, a student who had just given his life to Christ lost his life in a tragic car accident. This shocked our entire school and quickened my passion to see souls saved. I was still emotionally shut down when it happened, but I was aware enough to watch how it had a major effect on my classmates. He was a true follower of Christ. Almost everywhere he went, he shared the love of Christ with people. This was evident to everyone at my school, and they were shocked that his life ended so suddenly.

The second thing happened shortly after that student died. Nobody was prepared for it. Two months later, another student was killed in a car accident. He was a great guy and a strong follower of Christ. His story especially affected me. I had known him personally and had spent some time with him. I was told he'd suffered nearly identical injuries as the ones I had suffered. This hit me like a ton of bricks. What was God saying to me? Why had I survived and he hadn't?

At the time, I didn't know exactly why I had survived my accident, but I knew God wanted me to learn something from these fatal car accidents. How was it possible that just a few months before, I was declared a fatality? It became clear to me that God had a greater purpose for me to accomplish than what I could see with my own eyes.

These two young men were not much different from me, yet they had lost their lives. They would never come back to school, and I had been given a second chance at life. Why? I couldn't figure it out. I remember feeling guilty that I had survived and these two great young men had not. I now know that was a false guilt. I felt even more guilt after overhearing a classmate say they didn't understand why they died and I had lived. After that, I felt as if my whole high school was upset that I had lived and those two young men had not.

Almost daily, after these two tragedies in our school, I would here various prayer requests and announcements made citing newspaper reports about young people who had lost their lives in horrific car accidents near our small town. I remember going home in shock and wondering what to do with all of it. I felt as if God was revealing part of my purpose to me. I wrote about how I felt burdened for the many people who might be in a car crash and must face their eternity without ever having made peace with God. I looked at many of the students in my high school who went back to their normal, carefree lives after a little grieving over the two young men. I was burdened for them as well; I knew so many were caught up in their little worlds and numb to what should have been sobering truths for all of us.

I made up my mind that the passing of those two young men, as well as the numerous tragedies I heard about in class, would be a constant memory and motivating force in me to declare the truth of God's love to as many hopeless people as I could. I wasn't quite cognitively aware of what it all meant, but I knew God was telling me something significant. He wanted me to know how delicate our lives are and that they can end in a moment. I could have easily been the third student in my school who lost his life. As time went on, I realized God wasn't calling me to a normal life to be lived for my own fulfillment; my life was truly not my own. God had determined my destiny, and I had to give up the idea of a normal life in order to embrace what God was preparing me for.

Another big lesson I learned from this was "*the effectual prayer of a righteous man avails much*" (James 5:16). I had always heard that if I put my faith in God, He would answer my prayers. However,

I had never personally experienced how God is true to His word until He revealed Himself as my healer and restorer.

I now realize that this whole concept of purpose is so intricately tied to whether we live solely for ourselves or not. In retrospect, I can see that God wanted me to realize how fleeting our lives are, but there was another lesson to be learned: God has given each of us a unique purpose to fulfill on this earth, and we can experience joy and peace when we are truly walking in our destiny. However, the key is that we simply cannot live out of our own selfish motives. If my high school had realized this right after the two tragic car accidents, they would not have returned to the same state of complacency and selfishness they were in before both tragic events. The Bible says people will be in a stupor during the last days. I believe we're in that time.

God wanted me to see the beauty and fulfillment of walking in His plan for me, but He also wanted me to see it selflessly. I may not have fully understood at the time, but God was trying to get me to understand that to truly impact a generation and to truly touch lives for the kingdom of God, I would have to resolve myself that my own interests and desires must be put away, and I was to live selflessly for God's glory and for the benefit of lost, broken, and hurting people.

With the help of God — and my teachers — I finally finished my senior year. I graduated with honors. Many doctors said it was medically impossible for my brain to retain what I learned. But God.

CHAPTER 13

CROSS COUNTRY

I trained the entire summer, as I headed to the trails each day with my dog, Buddy. When I would fall, he would stop and wait for me to get up and resume our run. We were running buddies that entire summer. He too was a huge cheerleader for me. In his own way, he would tell me to get up and press in every time I fell. It was almost a three-mile run around the field behind our house. I would run a little, fall, pray, and then regain my strength and get back up. I had to build up my endurance to complete the first mile. I knew God was giving me strength to keep going. Falling was discouraging, but when I felt the strength to get back up, I was encouraged, got up, and kept going.

It wasn't until a month later that I could run a mile without falling. I would come home out of breath and drenched with sweat. On many occasions, I would sneak in the downstairs door so my mom wouldn't see how bad my knees were bleeding from the falls. But I pressed on to the second and third miles after that.

By the fall of my junior year, I was able to get back on the team. That was an exciting yet extremely hard season. Everyone knew I had struggled, but just being on the team gave me a sense of accomplishment.

I had overcome the hall, then the backyard, and the first three miles around the field behind our house. Now it was time to hit the road. Could I do it? Yes! With Buddy by my side, I reached my seven-mile goal. This was a huge goal to reach, and it prepared me for my first cross country meet. It took me much longer than I thought, but I didn't let that stop me. Each race, my timing increased and my falls lessened. I felt my body strengthen, and as I prayed each morning, I knew my spirit was getting strong enough to enter my first race.

I didn't have any idea how hard getting back on that cross country team would be. It was a challenge, but I forced and disciplined myself. I learned to not give in to any negative thoughts. If I had a passion to run, I was going to overcome every obstacle. I would not quit! I had the will to persevere. It was a desire of my heart, and though it seemed impossible and the doctors had told my parents I would not be able to do such activities, I disciplined my body and had faith in God to do what seemed impossible. As I trained with the team, I quoted verses like Philippians 4:13, *"I can do all things through Christ who strengthens me!"* I even watched *Rocky* movies and gained inspiration from his determination. I would see myself running and crossing the finish line. With God's help, I knew He would allow me to cross every finish line that He had prepared for me.

The day for the first meet arrived. I was nervous, but I decided that, no matter how I placed, I would stay grateful just for having the opportunity to be on a team again. A glimpse of the finish line kept me motivated.

The long-awaited race arrived. I was competing against sixty people. I started off strong, but when I fell the first time, it was a hard fall. Cut and bleeding, I got up, but the fall had set me back. I started running again, but I was disoriented and began to run in the wrong direction; yes, I got off the path and ran into another field like Forest Gump. When some of the runners saw me, they yelled and got my attention. It was embarrassing, but I didn't let it completely shut me down. I hadn't come this far to quit because of embarrassment. I made my way back across the field and got on the right path. At that point, I thought many times about getting off track and how I had to battle so many fears, but God's voice was much stronger within my spirit.

I finished eleventh out of sixty runners. My knees were cut and bleeding from the multiple falls. I was gasping for breath and about to pass out. I had to be taken to the medic tent, but I didn't care. By the grace of God, I'd done it! Another finish line had been conquered.

That day, as I crossed the finish line, I knew I would receive God's promise that someday I would be able to run my full race without being weary.

> *"But they that wait upon the Lord shall renew their strength; they shall mount up with wings as eagles; they shall run, and not be weary; and they shall walk, and not faint."* –
> *Isaiah 40:31*

CHAPTER 14

GRADUATION

I was honored when my school asked me to speak to my class at my graduation commencement ceremony. As I prepared the speech, God brought it all together for me. I could see things clearly.

I still walked with a limp. I was wobbly and unsure as I walked up the steps and across the stage. I couldn't believe I was there, standing before my graduating class. I still talked very slowly and had difficulty pronouncing many of my words. I was still in recovery from the horrific accident that almost took my life, but three years later, I was addressing my senior class. It was an undeniable representation of God's mighty healing power.

As I looked out at the crowd of over one thousand people, I experienced a wave of mixed emotions. I saw my parents and grandparents in the front row; I knew they loved and supported me. A few rows back, I saw one of my favorite therapists, Shauna, the one who helped me take my first steps and taught me to walk again. In the back was my physical therapy doctor, Dr. Drew, who coached me as I learned to run again. Then there were all my teachers, the ones who had supported me. They knew how hard I had worked, and they celebrated my success.

Then I saw the faces of my classmates. I still couldn't understand why some of them who had once liked me, mocked me after the accident. For some of them, I had been the center of their jokes for the last two years. It was a painful two years. I went from being one of the popular guys on campus to being the object of ridicule.

As I walked up on the stage and faced my peers, I knew I was only there because God had helped me overcome countless obstacles. It was not a time to get even, nor was it a time to tell them how badly they had hurt me. God had given me the opportunity to speak on His behalf.

One of my favorite teachers introduced me. I was delighted because he was one of the few who had visited me in the hospital. I slowly began to address my senior class.

I challenged my class to not leave the safe haven of that Christian school—where they had been served everything they needed on a platter—just to go out into the world and forget what they had learned. I challenged them to not just live for themselves. I challenged them to live every day as if it could be their last day on earth.

I closed with these final words:

"Live your life for Christ. Live each day of your life as if that day is the last day instead of the first day of the rest of your life. You are here for a purpose greater than yourself; make a difference in this world every day. All our lives are uncertain. Only what we do for Christ will last."

I gave God all the glory. While I was addressing my class, I thought of the two young men from my school who had died. The accident I endured and their shortened lives led me to tell my class to live selflessly, live with a purpose, and live passionately.

It was awesome—I even got a standing ovation. And I was honored and blessed by God to receive the Solio de Gloria award.

CHAPTER 15

I FOUND MY JEWEL

After graduating from high school, I went on to take a few classes at a local junior college. As with everything in my recovery journey, this took me longer than I had expected. But, again, I learned that I was being prepared to run the race and win. You don't win without hard work and determination.

I remember during that time after graduation, I would spend hours upon hours listening to a Jesus Culture podcast from the Jesus Culture Awakening Chicago 2011 concert and crying out for this generation. Banning Liebscher would preach on the podcast, and my heart was ignited and would be so burdened for this generation. I would listen to his messages on the podcast over and over and over again, and my hunger for God and desire to see this generation awakened grew.

Through junior college, I was being prepared to face life on my own at Liberty University. This is where I met the love of my life and my jewel,

Mariah. She would not only run cross country with me; she would be the one who God called to run alongside me to awaken this generation.

I had been praying for years for God to give me a God-honoring, humble, and sweet wife, kind of like Ruth Graham was to Billy Graham. Billy Graham was and is a hero of mine, and I thought it would be great to find a young lady with a heart for ministry and characteristics similar to Ruth Graham. I prayed and waited, and prayed and waited for years. All throughout high school and during my time in community college, I would get on my knees at night and plead to God, asking Him to bring me a Godly, humble young lady with whom I could spend my life serving God.

I remember listening to Banning Liebscher preach on the podcast, saying, "Just say 'yes' to Jesus," "Jesus requires your entire life," and, "Nations of the earth will be changed because of your life." I remember dropping to my knees and praying, "Jesus, I give You my entire life. Please take my life and use me to impact this generation. Send me a young lady who will love You as I love You, and we will serve You together."

Finally, around my junior year of college at Liberty University, in February 2013, God answered my prayers. The next day at the convocation, where ministry majors attended, I walked into the auditorium to hear the worship band playing. I smiled and started singing one of the songs as I looked for a seat. I was just minding my own business, trying to find a seat.

Suddenly, I looked over and saw this sweet blonde girl sitting all alone. Something about her was special and unique. She seemed different and set apart and more mature and Godly than any girl I had ever seen. So I thought, *Well, I can just sit beside her!* And indeed I did. I walked over and sat down, and I kind of introduced myself. She was quiet and shy, so she just smiled at me. When the worship songs ended, Dr. Dave Wheeler came on stage and told everyone to turn to their neighbor and introduce themselves and ask if they needed prayer for anything. I don't remember Mariah saying she needed prayer for anything, but from talking to her for a minute, I could tell Mariah was a very special and Godly girl. I could tell she was different from all the other girls at Liberty. Since I had already introduced myself to Mariah, I turned to her, had a little small talk, and asked if she was free after convocation. She said she was free. So I asked Mariah to go get coffee at Barnes and Noble.

After convocation, we walked to get coffee and talked as we went. All I remember is she got hot chocolate instead of coffee and still, to this day, she doesn't drink coffee. She has told me that she never agreed to go out with a guy while at Liberty, but something prompted her to go with me.

That night, Mariah sent me a friend request on Facebook. Of course, I accepted. I had forgotten to get her phone number when we were at Barnes and Noble, so I was overjoyed she found me on Facebook. We began to converse via Messenger, and I quickly learned where she sat in regular convocation. I would go see her quickly before every convocation started. We decided to go to Washington, DC together for a day. Wow, what a trip! That was one of the most enjoyable and memorable trips of my life. She actually parked next to a fire hydrant and got a parking ticket, but I sneakily grabbed the ticket and paid it. After this day, it was obvious that I liked her.

After that, we went to a Third Day concert together and then started seeing each other regularly. I was thrilled when I learned she was a missionary kid who had been ministering with her family in Africa. The reason I was so excited was I had always prayed for God to allow me to find a missionary kid like Ruth Graham had been. I was overjoyed that God had lead me to find such a precious jewel.

When summer break came, I went back home to North Carolina, and she went back to South Africa to be with her family. Over that summer, we communicated through Facebook and got to know each other even more. I told my family I believed I had found the jewel of all jewels. At that time, we were just friends. I knew I liked her, but I couldn't tell if she really liked me. Yet, something in me told me to keep pursuing her.

The following semester, we talked even more. We kept seeing each other much more as well. I would always go visit her at her seat in convocation before the speaker started. Then I asked her if she would ride home with me to meet my family, and she agreed to. I was so excited for my family to meet her that I didn't think the weekend would ever come. When we arrived, I had another surprise! I found out she loved cross country running as much as I did. That weekend, we ran together for the first time; it was great to finally have a real running partner.

I invited her to come visit with my family and I again the next weekend. During that weekend, we skyped her parents from South Africa, and I asked her dad for permission to date her. To my relief, he said, "Yes, we trust Mariah's judgment in who she chooses to date."

And so, we began our official dating relationship. Mariah was my best friend, and we did everything together, including hiking and running. I loved that she enjoyed the same things that I did.

We ended up dating for three years. There were a couple bumps along the way, and I waited long enough to propose to make sure each of us had enough time to prepare and be spiritually and emotionally ready before we got married. I also wanted to make absolutely certain that I was in God's will and not reacting purely on emotions.

I wanted this to be a well thought-out and prayed-out decision. Also, I needed to have the money for the engagement ring — and maturity as a man of God. I knew marriage was a super big deal and not something to be taken lightly, so I needed to make sure I was ready in my heart and prepared to enter into a covenant, a sacred marriage relationship with Mariah.

I knew I loved Mariah and we were to be together for the rest of our lives. But a brain injury can cause you to do funny things. I proposed and then took the ring back the same day. What? Yes! My brain panicked and told me I wasn't ready and I needed to wait. As I calmed myself down and spent some alone time with God, I knew I loved her and wanted to marry her. I learned from that experience not to give in to brain panic. Brain panic releases emotions that are out of control. This taught me that when I have brain panic from a decision, I must spend time with God, try to hear His voice, and let Him lead my heart. I can't always rely on just what my feelings tell me; I have to trust in God.

After that episode, I was amazed that Mariah chose to still love me! I really saw her spiritual maturity and depth of character. I restored the relationship with Mariah; I knew I had messed up big time and had really hurt her. Man, I was embarrassed and felt like trash! I told her I was so sorry, asked for her forgiveness, and told her I wasn't ending our engagement.

I am still a little embarrassed about it, and I even struggled with including it in this chapter. I knew I messed up, and I repented to God for hurting the precious jewel that He had blessed me with. I asked Him to forgive me for acting in such a selfish way. I am so glad that I serve the God of second chances. He heard my prayer of repentance and remembered it no more.

I am so thankful that God led me to her, that He led me to sit beside her on that day in ministry convocation, introduce myself to her, and ask her out for coffee. I am thankful she chose to go to ministry convocation that day, because she usually did not. I am thankful for the heart of love she had for me that kept her from breaking up with me after that first proposal.

When I proposed the second and official time, I really did it the right way. I took her to a very special place near Linville falls in North Carolina. There was a small waterfall, a small pool of still water, and a large rock in the middle of the stream. When we went to this place, I could feel something special in the atmosphere. It was almost as if

God had led me to this special place beside the still water so that I could take Mariah to the solid rock, to propose to her besides the beautiful waterfall.

I had found this place before, and I took her to this beautiful area with excitement. To me, maybe to nobody else, this place represented the strength of a solid rock in Christ, the peaceful, still waters to which God leads us beside, and the Living Water — the waterfall — of God's love, which is always available through a relationship with Jesus Christ. With great excitement, I took her to the rock beside the waterfall, knelt down, and asked her to marry me. I wanted the rock to symbolize that we were founding our marriage on the solid rock of Jesus Christ. I knew that only if our marriage was founded on the love of Christ, we would we have a great, lasting marriage.

This time was different. With a huge smile and tears running down her face, she said "Yes, of course!" We were so excited, and immediately on the drive home, we began making our plans for the wedding. We laughed, made plans, and dreamed of that amazing day!

Our wedding day seemed to come so fast. What ended up being about eight or nine months seemed like just a month. We were so excited that we barely noticed the time. Though we did not like the time, I felt like the length of time added an extra excitement to our wedding day. It was worth the wait. Mariah and I met with a few mentors and counselors to help us work through some premarital things. I am glad we had an extended engagement to work on these issues. However, when we married, we were both very much ready, mentally, spiritually, psychologically, and emotionally.

There was a ton of planning that went into the wedding. I wanted our wedding day to symbolize a marriage founded on Jesus Christ, so I had an old rugged cross my family had used for decades in ministry put on stage so we could kneel at the cross and dedicate our lives and marriage to Jesus Christ.

> *Isaiah 55:10-11 says,*
> *As the rain and the snow come down from heaven, and do not return to it without watering the earth and making it bud and flourish, so that it yields seed for the sower and bread for the eater, so is my word that goes out from my mouth: It will not return to me empty, but will accomplish what I desire and achieve the purpose for which I sent it.*

CHAPTER 16

FORGIVENESS IS THE KEY

Forgiving others was the major key to my recovery. I discovered that the more I worked through forgiving those I blamed for the accident, the more I recovered.

This was the most amazing discovery! Could it be that forgiveness is a key that unlocks our destiny? For me, it was; forgiveness turned my tragedy into triumph.

Your door of destiny could be right in front of you, but until you use the key of forgiveness, you may never be able to unlock the door and walk through it.

Without forgiveness, we stay trapped in and tormented by our past. Our past becomes a prison that we never get out of until we walk through the door that God has provided. Jesus said, "I am the door" (John 10:7).

He is the door that we must go through to enter into our destiny, and forgiveness is the key that opens this door. Jesus's final miracle made the way for everyone to walk through Him in order to reach their destiny. He modeled for us the way to use the key when He forgave those who had persecuted Him as He hung on the cross in agony. He then declared in John 19:30, "It is finished!" His declaration of forgiveness modeled for us how forgiveness should take place. Had Jesus not forgiven, He would not have been the perfect lamb of God. Even Jesus had to use the key of forgiveness in His worst moment of pain and agony on earth. Heaven was Jesus's destination, and He had to use the key of forgiveness to show us how to forgive our enemies. Jesus is the door and He has provided us salvation when we place our faith and belief in Him. He has also provided freedom from bondage when we forgive those who hurt, criticize, or mistreated us.

When we don't quickly forgive those who have hurt us, we form judgments, and bitterness takes over and locks us up in the pain of our past.

In Matthew 6:14, Jesus said, "*For if you forgive men their trespasses, your heavenly Father will also forgive you.*"

My recovery was hanging on my forgiveness and I had so many unanswered questions.

My first question was, "Why did my sister pull out when she couldn't see clearly?" My second was, "Why didn't dad come with us on our trip?" If he had been driving, the accident would have not happened as it did. My third was, "Why did my mom allow my eighteen-year-old sister to drive?" And lastly, "Why did the semi driver wave us out into traffic with another semi fast approaching and then drive off as if nothing happened?"

Well, these questions may never be answered, but I couldn't let these unanswered questions stop my forgiveness. I started with my sister. She was the first one I had to work to forgive. Not many people understand the power of forgiveness, but Jesus told us how often to forgive. In Matthew 18, Jesus tells us not to forgive just seven times, but seventy times seven. It is a continuous process of forgiveness. It took days, nights, months, and even years to work through my list. And many times, I would pray over and over again until I had truly forgiven. I had to continually choose to forgive my sister. Yes, she had pulled out in front of the semi when my mom said, "wait" and yes I had a right to be angry at her. However, I continually would make the choice to pray and forgive her, even when those feelings of anger would come back to my heart and mind. There were things she may have done after the accident that I was angry at her for, and I could have stayed angry at her. However, I continually would pray, "Lord Jesus, I choose to forgive her. I release her from the prison of my heart." The restoration of my relationship with my sister was not instant, but a marathon, a gradual process of persevering to forgive.

Forgiving my dad took longer than any of the others. I looked up to my dad, and before the accident, he had been my best friend. We did everything together. But the day I asked him to go on the trip with us, he had something more important to do; he had to work. It took years to process how that had wounded me. I had to really work to forgive him by praying many times and processing it with different counselors, especially my mom. I could feel my anger, and I knew I had not completely forgiven him. I resented that he chose work over going with the family on spring break that year. But what I was not realizing was that each time I would work through another layer of forgiveness, I would regain something I had lost due to the accident. I would regain mobility or speech or even a skill I had lost. God was working, drawing me to face my pain and deal with it His way. And that way is to forgive. I couldn't wait until I understood why I had to forgive out of obedience to God, but if we wait until we understand why someone does something that hurts us, we can remain trapped in that pain for a lifetime.

As I reflect back, I realize that it has taken me close to twelve years to completely forgive my dad for not being there for me for just twelve hours of my life. I was only fatherless for twelve hours!

For those who have been fatherless for twelve years of their life, I know the pain must be unbearable at times. I believe the enemy's most successful trap is to convince us that what we have suffered from is too great and the person who caused us to suffer doesn't deserve to be forgiven. This is one of the enemy's most successful lies. He knows we stand at the door of our destiny and if we don't use the key to unlock the door, we can remain trapped in the pain of our past for a lifetime.

When we forgive others, we free ourselves from the prison of unforgiveness. For me, I can say that once I grabbed ahold of forgiveness, I began to get out of the prison of the paralyzed body in which I was trapped. The more I forgave, the more I was able to regain my normal movements.

During that time of my journey through forgiveness (a journey I'm still navigating), I was confronted with the real reason an unforgiving spirit couldn't reside in me. God spoke to me through a pastor friend. He said many people have a calling, but my calling was a higher calling. He said God was not going to let me get by with an unforgiving, bitter spirit. He said I would be miserable, and I had too much to do for God's kingdom to allow bitterness to defeat me. Those words resonated with me then, and they echo in my heart to this day. God was warning me about the far-reaching, negative consequences of bitterness — a warning I heed every day.

The author of Hebrews talks about how destructive bitterness can be in our lives and the lives of those around us. In Hebrews 12:15, we read "looking carefully lest anyone fall short of the grace of God; lest any root of bitterness springing up cause trouble, and by this many become defiled;" A root of bitterness will cause chaos in your life and the lives of those around you.

On the cross, Jesus forgave all who were responsible for His sufferings. He forgave during the time of His worst excruciating pain and suffering. He never allowed bitterness to get control of His heart. He simply forgave, even when those who nailed Him to the cross refused to apologize. He provided forgiveness for all sins through His shed blood. Through His actions, Jesus showed us how to forgive others in the mist of the pain. Then He said, "It is finished!"

If you still feel the pain from something someone did that caused harm, pray the following prayer daily:

A Prayer to Forgive

Dear Heavenly Father,
I need Your help to forgive _____
for_____. The pain is still very real to me. I
have not been able to forgive because my thoughts are
always on what they did and how much they hurt me.
Today, as I feel this pain, I choose to forgive
_____for_____. Thank you that I
don't have to pretend that their actions did not hurt
me. I ask You to heal my heart and remove this pain.
Where the hurt and pain was in my heart, I ask that
You would fill me with Your love and heal the wound.
I choose to be obedient to Your Word and release them
from their debt. I forgive them for _____ and for
the pain their actions have caused me.
Father God forgive me of the bitterness in my heart
towards_____ for_____.
Father, I choose to release them. I accept the shed blood
of Jesus as payment for their sin. They owe me nothing.
Jesus, You shed Your blood for their sins as well as mine.
Forgive me for my sinful responses of anger. Now, I ask
that You wash my heart clean of the resentment.
In Jesus's Name,
Amen.

CHAPTER 17

A FORTY-HOUR LABOR

On the morning of August 29th, 2017, Mariah began to have serious pain in her abdomen and womb. I knelt beside her and held her hand as she groaned in very uncomfortable pain. She was in the early signs of labor for the birth of our beautiful baby girl, Elizabeth Grace Boggs. We labored the first part at home before driving to the hospital to deliver.

I stayed by Mariah's side and held her hand the entire time. I felt her pain and agony as I watched her. She initially tried to deliver Elizabeth naturally, with no epidural or pain meds. She was a first-time mom, so we were both new to everything. The first baby is always the hardest labor.

We had been going to a natural birthing center for a lot of pre-birth consultations and even some training, and the midwives from that birthing center were even there to encourage us, coach Mariah as she labored, and help deliver our baby into the world. However, after thirty-two hours of labor, the pain became unbearable. Mariah gave in and had to have some pain meds and an epidural. I didn't blame her. It was almost making me sick watching how much pain she was in. We were all relieved to see some of her pain subside when she received the pain meds and epidural. She said the epidural helped, but it really did not lessen much of the labor pain of delivering Elizabeth. Eight hours later, Elizabeth was born late at night on the 30th.

Everyone had told us a truth about when the baby comes out, but we got to experience it first-hand. When the baby finally comes out, all the pain of childbirth pretty much leaves, except for some of the soreness afterwards.

The reward and beauty of our baby girl made all the pain and suffering Mariah had gone through worth it. I understood the passage of Galatians 4:19 a little more, where Paul writes, "My little children for whom I labor in birth again until Christ is formed in you." The Greek word for "formed" is also *metamorphoo*, which has a very similar meaning to metamorphosis. Sometimes before Christ is truly formed in us, or until we truly become Christ-like, we go through some testing and some dark, hard, or lonely places for a season. A caterpillar must go through the dark place of the cocoon before the beautiful butterfly that God created it to be can come forth. If anybody else tries to help the caterpillar get out, it will die. The caterpillar must go through the process of getting out of the dark cocoon alone. Before we were able to experience and enjoy our beautiful baby girl, Mariah had to suffer in labor. Beauty came after the immense pain.

I do not believe that God causes any type of suffering in our lives, but He does allow certain things to happen to mold us and shape us. Just like in the biblical stories of Joseph and Job, God allows His children to go through certain trials, but He does not cause suffering. God will never leave one of His children alone in the turmoil he or she is in. He allows the hurt, pain, and conflict to mold an individual and draw that person closer to Himself. He will always provide a way of escape from the pain and suffering. As we read in 2 Corinthians 3:18, usually, if not all the time, God will bring the individual who has experienced a considerable amount of suffering to a place of glory, recompense, and more purpose afterwards. It is always God's intent to use the dark, hard times in the cocoon to cause His children to be transformed into the image of Jesus and bring them to new levels of glory. It is only after the suffering and in the ashes that the beauty of the butterfly of who he or she really is, can blossom forth. There is purpose in the pain. A key, however, is that one must not grow bitter or angry. Joseph and Job would not have been recompensed if they had stayed bitter or angry. I don't believe I would have progressed and been recompensed like I have if I had stayed stuck in anger, bitterness, or unforgiveness.

Mariah and I had to persevere through forty hours of labor before our beautiful baby girl, Elizabeth, was born into the world.

CHAPTER 18

WHAT IS MY PURPOSE?

The most important question we can ask is: *"What is my purpose?"* People spend their entire lives trying to find the answer without asking the only One who knows it. Philosophers and theologians have debated purpose since the beginning of time. The truth is everyone on this planet has a purpose. God is the only One who knows why He created each of us, and we must seek Him for the answer.

I believe God began revealing my purpose to me before the car accident. After the accident, though, He showed me there were areas in my life that I needed to understand. I had to understand how forgiveness works so I could overcome unforgiveness and not get stuck in bitterness. I had to understand how to resist self-pity so I could fully embrace the faith to walk in my purpose.

When the accident occurred, my life changed in an instant. Did I suffer? Yes, I suffered, but my purpose was greater than the circumstances — greater than an eighteen-wheeler.

As I have been reading more books by Banning Liebscher, I really like what Banning says about Joseph in his book *Rooted*:

> Joseph, a man of God, who God used to save the entire nation of Israel knew he had a purpose. But, he did not know the preparation and trials he would have to go through before God allowed the initial seed planted in his life as a young boy, to produce fruit. Joseph had to be deeply rooted in his relationship with his Heavenly Father so that the pain and suffering did not embitter him and thwart the plans and purposes God had for him. Joseph did not know that he would need to go through thirteen years of trials and testing, before God allowed the greatness in his life to come forth (Liebscher 4).

In a similar way, I had to persevere through thirteen years of suffering. God has fully recompensed me for my loss and has blessed me with full recovery, a beautiful wife, and a daughter (Elizabeth). I am secure and rooted in the fullness of God's love, with a clear sense of His plan and purposes for my life and family.

Many seeds had been planted in me before my accident. I remember how I would spend hours reading the Word. I believe I had a desire to reach this generation, yet I did not know what I would have to go through before that seed would bear fruit in my life.

As Banning Liebscher talks about in his book *Rooted*, "Those men and women in the Bible who achieved greatness were the ones who were rooted in God, but who also went through a time of preparation" (Liebscher 4).

God first planted a seed in them, but before He brought them to the place of greatness where they would make Him famous, they were first famous in the secret place — that place of intimacy with Jesus. They had to be rooted in Him, and then there was the process of God growing them to become the men and women of God He had called them to be (Liebscher 4).

I want to encourage you to believe that God has a purpose for your life too. I want you to know as you forgive those you have blamed for any hardships or hurts from which you have suffered, you will progress toward your purpose. The door to your destiny will be unlocked. Had I not forgiven those I blamed for the accident, I would not be walking in victory today. I have seen the miraculous hand of God move in my life, and I want you to know He will move in your life too.

If you are suffering from a sickness, a disease, or an injury such as mine (TBI), God's healing power is for you, if you will place your faith and belief in His healing power. Yes, healing is for you! God, through His Son, Jesus Christ, offers salvation and healing today to anyone who will receive it.

God did not bring me back to life and keep me on this earth for no reason; He brought me back to declare hope to the hopeless. It is my passion to take the life He gave me and use it for His glory.

I pray I have inspired you to believe in the God of Miracles! To believe that He loves you and that whatever you are facing right now, you can overcome. You weren't just created; you were created with a divine purpose, and with God's help, you can overcome every obstacle. Take one obstacle at a time, pray, and believe, and as you persevere, you too can discover and walk in your God-given purpose.

I spoke earlier of how Jesus is the door, but maybe you don't know how to forgive because you have never opened that door and asked Jesus to forgive you of your sin. You may have never received the free gift of salvation through placing your belief and faith in the death, burial, and resurrection of Jesus Christ. Maybe the reason you have struggled finding your purpose is that you have never come to know the only One who truly gives us purpose when we place our faith in His Son, Jesus Christ, and ask Him to cleanse us from our sins. In John 14:6, Jesus said, *"I am the Way, the truth, and the life. No one comes to the Father except through Me."*

If you haven't placed your belief and faith in Jesus Christ, the only way to Salvation and God, and asked Him to forgive you of your sins and to become your Savior, I encourage you to not go another day without crying out to Jesus for your salvation. Ask Him to cleanse you of your sins and to forgive you of choosing your way over His way. It's never too late for a lost sinner to come to Jesus. If today you don't know Him, let today be the first day of the rest of your life with Jesus Christ as your Lord and Savior!

If you have never done so and are ready to receive Christ as your Lord and Savior, then pray the following prayer:

Lord Jesus, I confess and ask You to forgive me for how I have chosen my way over Yours. Please forgive me of my sins, and cleanse me with Your blood. Thank you, Lord Jesus, for dying on the cross for my sins, and I accept Your death, burial, and resurrection as payment for my sins. I place my faith and trust in You for my salvation, and I ask You to become Lord and Savior of my life. I surrender to You.

Thank you, Jesus, amen.

I promise you, if you prayed that prayer and meant it with all your heart, then Christ is now Your Savior, and you are my brother or sister in Christ! I encourage you to find a Bible-believing church, so you can be discipled by a pastor, grow with other believers, and discover that you too have an Unshakable Destiny.

If you received Christ for the first time, please let us know at Living Waters Ministry by writing to 4803 Old Vashti Rd. Hiddenite, NC, or emailing us at unshakabledestinybook@gmail.com.

God bless your journey!

William Boggs IV

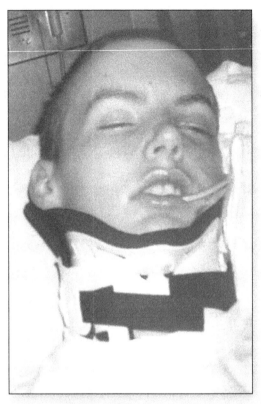

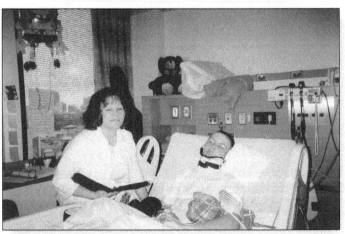

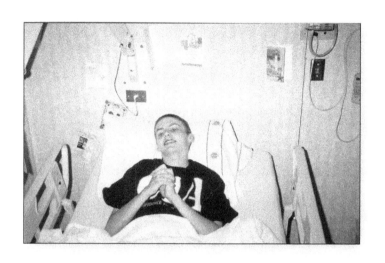

Family receives an outpouring of love and help

Support ranges from money and visits to group prayer

BY KATIE PARSLEY
KPARSLEY@STATESVILLE.COM

Three weeks after a semi truck slammed into his family's car, 15-year-old William Boggs is still fighting for his life.

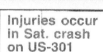

Boggs

Severe brain injuries have kept the Statesville Christian School ninth-grader in a coma since the day before Easter. He's making progress, though doctors say it could be months longer.

"It's a slow process. It's truly a miracle he's alive," said his mother, Denise. "It's a miracle we're all alive."

William, his mother and his sister, Casey, were traveling to his grandparents' home in Florida when the accident occurred. Denise and Casey were treated for cuts and bruises, but William remains unconscious in a Jacksonville hospital.

The family has stayed with him for the past 20 days, sleeping in the Ronald McDonald House and keeping vigil at his bedside. But they haven't been alone.

Hundreds of friends and family have called, e-mailed or made the hours-long trip to visit.

See **BOGGS**, *Page* **3A**

Injuries occur in Sat. crash on US-301

Three North Carolina residents were injured Saturday evening in a traffic crash on US-301 north of Starke.

A 2001 Isuzu, driven by Casey D. Boggs, 19, of Stony Point, N.C., was crossing the northbound lanes of US-301 from Northeast 193th Street, according to Florida Highway Patrol Trooper Jason Barry. The Isuzu failed to yield for northbound traffic and was struck in the side by a 2001 semi, Trooper Barry said.

Boggs and passengers Denise Boggs, 47, and William L. Boggs, 15, were life-flighted from the scene. William Boggs' injuries were serious.

As the Isuzu was struck the spare tire broke free and struck a 2002 Dodge on the driver's side door. The Dodge, driven by Evany L. Green, 23, of Jacksonville, was southbound. Trooper Barry said.

No injuries were listed for Green and passengers Brittney Davis, 23, and Marria Davis, 3, both of Jacksonville and semi driver Brenda Allen, 47,

123

BOGGS: *Class and church have raised thousands*

Continued from Page 1

Thousands more have sent cards and promised to pray for his recovery.

"It's been really overwhelming," said William's father, Lou. "We didn't realize we had this many friends who cared about us."

William's classmates at Statesville Christian School have been among the most dedicated supporters. They've sent countless e-mails and cards, and they begin each class with a prayer for their friend.

"We've poured our hearts out to God," said 15-year-old Sydney Andrews. "We want him to get better."

The kids say class isn't the same without William, who's known for his sense of humor and love of Wranglers. They say he's more likely to be running or singing than sitting still.

His friend Justin Mills calls him a human jukebox. Teachers call him a perfect student, and students call him a perfect friend.

"He's a rare gem," said Kresten Kuchipa, a freshman. "There's not too many people like him."

This is the first time a student from Statesville Christian has been in this kind of situation, according to guidance counselor Brian Pestotnik, and it's brought the school together.

"It's been quite a shock," Pestotnik said. "This is a very godly young man, very respectful. It makes you ask how such a good kid can go through such a tragic event."

Students and parents have tried to help in any way they can, including raising money to pay for William's medical bills. Along with his church, Shiloh Tabernacle, they have collected enough to pay for the $6,000 flight that will bring him to Charlotte on Monday.

Once William arrives at Charlotte Institute of Rehabilitation, specialists will attempt to bring him out of the coma. He's already gone from a Stage 3 coma — when a patient is at the point of death — to a state of near-consciousness.

He's still not completely out, but he does something different every day, that encourages us," Denise said. "Every little thing is just a miracle."

William can snap his fingers on command and can open his eyes for short periods of time. His heartbeat in creases every time he sees a picture of his dog or horses.

Doctors can't say for sure if William will make a full recovery, but his mother says there have been several positive signs.

"I feel like he's slowly healing. God's moving in his body and changing things," Denise said. "There's no explanation when God does the healing."

The recovery process could take a month or a year, doctors say. Denise says she's sure her son will get better as quickly as possible.

"He's one of those kids who you never have to tell to do their homework. He does it every day, and he always goes over and beyond," she said. "I believe he'll do the same with his recovery. He's going to go over and beyond. His inner strength will sustain him."

MIRACLE: *Family owes $5.5 million in medical bills*

Continued from Page 1

Casey, who was driving, was treated for facial cuts and bruises. Denise suffered some bruising but was otherwise all right.

William was in a coma in critical condition for 18 days at a hospital in Jacksonville before he was airlifted to the Charlotte Institute of Rehabilitation, where specialists were able to bring him out of his coma.

Denise said the doctors told her that they had identified three injuries in William's brain and said any one of them could be fatal.

Doctors installed a bolt in William's head to monitor his brain activity and drain fluid, his mother said. His breathing was controlled by a respirator.

"The neurologist didn't give us much hope," Denise said. "He had severe brain damage."

While in the hospital in Florida, William had several surgeries that left his left side partially paralyzed and led doctors to believe that he may never walk again.

Two weeks ago, he began to slowly regain movement in his left side," Denise said. "It's truly a miracle. It has been a miracle unfolding the whole time."

Because of the brain injury, William had to relearn simple things like tying his shoes and walking. The former cross-country runner hopes that he will be running once again.

He has a chance at a full recovery," his father said.

William will undergo at least eight weeks of intensive physical therapy, and doctors say it will take at least a year for his brain to heal.

Crystal Dillon, William's nurse, said he had to relearn how to interact with people.

TYRONE SUMMERS / TSUMMERS@STATESVILLE.COM
William Boggs (far left) flashes his signature sign to friends and family during a welcome-home reception Wednesday with his dad, Lou, at his side.

During his hospital stay the others sparred with one nurse, but that was forgotten when he left the hospital Wednesday.

"He told her, 'I'll miss you,'" Dillon said. "At the door, he did a little dance. He's a funny kid and outgoing. He had all the nurses and therapists laughing."

The family's medical bills are about $5.5 million and became they were transitioning between insurance companies, they had no coverage at the time of the wreck.

James Dawson, a classmate at Statesville Christian School, described William's recovery as "pretty awesome."

He remembers visiting his friend in the hospital in Jacksonville when William wasn't eating or breathing on his own.

"Now he is here and talking and smiling," Dawson said. "It is amazing to see how far he has come."

Wednesday was the first time that friend Alex Bodin saw his classmate since school let out for spring break.

"He is in a better condition that I thought he'd be," Bodin said.

Lee said he is amazed at the love and support that has come from the community since the wreck.

"We have had e-mails from all over the country," he said. "Literally, within 24 hours of the accident, hundreds of people were praying for them."

Students from William's school came to visit him in the hospital and have raised money to support the family.

Justin Mills said news of William's accident shook him.

"I never thought it would happen to someone that close to me," he said.

William's mother has a word of advice for parents: "Take the time to spend with their kids and be a part of their lives. Life can be snatched away at any moment. Family is the most important thing."

Denise said the family owes a debt of thanks to Shiloh Tabernacle, Statesville Christian School and the entire community for their support.

'THE MIRACLE BOY'

Brain-damaged and paralyzed, William Boggs wasn't expected to live, let alone walk again. Now, the 15-year-old is back home and thriving

BY CARRIE J. SIDENER
CSIDENER@STATESVILLE.COM

Yellow balloons surrounded the Boggs' driveway each carrying messages like "Bless You All." The smell of sugar and chocolate wafted out of the kitchen.

There was a celebration on the carport, a celebration for William Boggs' life. The 15-year-old almost died 35 days ago when a tractor trailer slammed into his family's car during a spring break vacation, leaving him with severe brain injuries.

Weeks who was his first day home. His family say his recovery is a miracle.

"The first report that we had was that he had very little hope of even making it," said his father, Lee Boggs. "It is incredible to see him smile now. All I want to do now is spend time with him."

Lee and the doctors in Jacksonville, Fla., and Charlotte called William the "miracle boy."

"I'm just ready for life to get back to normal," William said Wednesday. "I feel great not to have to sleep in a hospital bed every day. And to have primary from all these nurses. And to have road trip."

The near-fatal accident occurred as William, his mother Denise and sister Casey were driving to Florida to spend spring break with his grandparents. Lee said it was something of a family tradition.

The family was already in Florida when a tractor trailer hit the back left side of the car, just behind where William was sitting.

When his mom arrived at the scene, William had no vital signs. He was at the same state when he arrived at the hospital.

"He was almost gone," his father said.

See MIRACLE, Page 7A

FAMILY'S MEDICAL BILLS TOTAL $5.5 MILLION

William's church, Shiloh Tabernacle, has is hard to help with expenses and is holding a benefit on June 25. There will be singing, games and barbecue. Call (704) 873-8877

Denise has also written about the wreck and her faith carried the family through. Visit www.livingwatersministry.us/testimony.html to read her account.

William Boggs pets his dog, Buddy, play Wednesday after coming home from the hospital. "I'm just ready for life to get back to normal," William says.

Lightning Source UK Ltd.
Milton Keynes UK
UKHW020707090123
415042UK00013B/2226